Donal McCann
Remembered

D0873686

Pat Laffan joined the Abbey Theatre in 1961 from University College Dublin, 'trained' on the boards with Donal McCann and performed in many plays with him during the 1960s. He has appeared in such films as *My Left Foot*, *The Snapper*, *The General*, *The Closer you Get* and *Country*. He is a director of the Gaiety School of Acting.

Faith O'Grady is a literary agent with the Lisa Richards Agency, Dublin.

Editors' Acknowledgements

The editors would like to thank all those who contributed to this book, and those who provided drawings and photos, especially Marguerite McGillicuddy, Brendan Sherry, Tom Lawlor and Bob Quinn. Special thanks to Donald Taylor Black who compiled the film and TV credits, and to Máiréad Delaney at the Abbey Theatre for her help with the theatre credits. We are very grateful to Ciara Considine and all at New Island Books, and to everyone at the Lisa Richards Agency for their support.

Image overleaf: Collage by Donal McCann containing many well-known faces from the arts, along with family members. Clockwise from left: Bob Quinn; Donal as Gabriel in The Dead; *Charlie Chaplin; Donal Donnelly; John Kavanagh; Donal as priest in* Budawanny; *Sean O'Casey; Joe Dowling; Donal as Captain Boyle in* Juno and the Paycock; *John Huston; Donal's younger brother who died in childhood; Donal's father in his confirmation suit; James Joyce.*

Donal McCann
Remembered

*To Ann
le gach dea ghuí.
Ó P. L.
12/9/2005.*

**EDITED BY PAT LAFFAN
& FAITH O'GRADY**

**NEW
ISLAND**

DONAL McCANN REMEMBERED
First published November 2000
New Island Books, 2 Brookside, Dundrum Road, Dublin 14

ISBN 1 902602 29 3

British Library Cataloguing in Publication Data
A catalogue record for this book is available
from the British Library

The Arts Council
An Chomhairle Ealaíon

New Island received financial assistance from The Arts Council
(An Chomhairle Ealaíon), Dublin, Ireland.

Grateful acknowledgement is made to the following individuals and organisations for permission to reproduce images, articles and other copyrighted material:

Dr Stephen Bowe; Donal Donnelly; John Fogarty; Tom Hickey; Pat Laffan; Tom Lawlor; John Lynch; Marguerite McGillicuddy; Barry McGovern; Maire Ní Ghráinne; photographers John Haynes and Tom Lawlor; Bob Quinn; Saskia Reeves; Brendan Sherry.

Film Ireland; *Film West*; Out of Joint Productions; The Estate of Katherine Kavanagh through The Jonathan Williams Literary Agency for permission to use an extract from 'Threshing Morning' by Patrick Kavanagh from *Selected Poems* ed. A. Quinn; The Gallery Press for permission to use an extract from *Faith Healer* by Brian Friel; The Harvill Press for permission to use an extract from *Christmas Day* by Paul Durcan; *The Irish Echo*; *The Irish Independent*; *The Irish Times*; *The Sunday Times*; *The Sunday Tribune*.

Cover design: Slick Fish Design, Dublin
Cover photograph: from *The Dead*, reproduced by permission of the
British Film Institute, London
Printed in Ireland by Colour Books, Dublin

3 5 4 2

Contents

Editors' Preface

The project began with a conversation between Lisa Cook, Faith O'Grady and myself shortly after Donal had died. Others considered it a worthy enterprise. Many friends, some no less vivid characters than Donal himself, agreed to participate. Some found it too difficult, too upsetting to do.

I feel sure that Donal would have approved of the project. His own contribution would have been witty or ironic. He would have made sure that you knew about his performance as the Cardinal of Uganda when he was twenty-two, leaving you in no doubt of the seriousness with which he approached his subject.

Many thanks to each of the contributors and congratulations on their promptness and their skill at this endeavour. Thanks to you the reader and, above all, thanks to Donal, who brought so much fun, affection and colour to all of us who knew him.

Pat Laffan, August 2000

I never met Donal McCann but I found his acting profoundly affecting. And as I have come to learn from talking to all those who kindly contributed to this book, his personality was as potent and compelling in real life as on stage or screen. I believe something of the complexity of the man has been captured in these pages, and I hope you, the reader, will find this too.

Faith O'Grady, October 2000

Ben Barnes

The Dancer and the Dance

I was not close to Donal McCann. He had that misplaced disdain for directors which sometimes afflict the prodigiously talented and whatever chance the men of his own time had — the likes of Joe Dowling and Max Stafford-Clark — fledglings of my generation were given polite (or sometimes not so polite) short shrift.

We knew each other quite well from the bear pit of Dublin theatre in the 1980s, but a measure of the mutual guardedness that characterised our encounters was thrown into sharp relief in poignant circumstances in the winter of 1991. Both our mothers were patients in Ely House in Wexford and while our paths often crossed on the polished linoleum floors in the hushed corridors where illness reigned, Donal and I never managed more than a grunted hello or a swift nod of acknowledgement as we made our separate ways to the sickbeds of our nearest and dearest. My mother died on the 27th of February that year and it was a measure of our sad reticence that that demise remained unacknowledged by Donal, and that to this day I do not know whether his own mother lived to re-cross the Slaney from Ferrybank.

And yet, for all that, I do not believe that I would be working in the theatre today but for Donal McCann. In 1980 I was entering my second year as a trainee director at the Abbey with little prospect of a breakthrough production on the horizon. Lots of assistant directing, play reading and wandering in and out of the big boys' technical and dress rehearsals. It was a dispiriting time when I was beginning to doubt my vocation and my staying power. On an August evening of that year I found myself in an empty auditorium with Brian Friel, Joe Dowling and Leslie Scott, attending the dress rehearsal of the first production of *Faith Healer*. Kate Flynn as Gracie, John Kavanagh as Teddy and, supremely, Donal McCann as Frank Hardy. It was a mesmeric experience to witness the word become flesh, to see the borderline between the art of the actor and the pain of the protagonist at first blur, then disappear. To watch the dancer become the dance. I was spellbound for two hours until he stepped forward into the light, removed his hat and spoke quietly into the dark of the auditorium:

> 'And as I moved across that yard towards them and offered myself to them, then for the first time I had a simple and genuine sense of homecoming. Then for the first time there was no atrophying terror and the maddening questions were silent. At long last I was renouncing chance.'

I saw the production ten times during its run at the Abbey and never again doubted the thrilling danger of the way or the courage of the wayfarers. I also never again doubted my need to be part of the alchemy of the theatre. Donal McCann and I did not have a decent conversation in twenty years of acquaintance but on that night, when he was in full possession of his great gift he was, for me, the faith healer of the flagging heart.

Ben Barnes is the Artistic Director of Abbey Theatre.

Line drawing by Donal McCann of the artist as Vladimir and Peter O'Toole as Estragon in *Waiting for Godot.*

Bernardo Bertolucci

Interview by Bob Quinn from the documentary, *It Must Be Done Right*

I was looking for an actor who was able to play an artist. Donal McCann entered and immediately I felt I had found this artist. Then I quickly tried to understand why I liked him so much. Why? He was almost bald, with very short hair. He looked a bit like a convict. I thought, What was I looking for from an actor to be an artist in the film? Looking at Donal, I understood it. I wanted this artist to have some colour of criminality. He could be a criminal. And the idea of artist as criminal — an artist is a criminal in society in some way, because an artist is in some way always very transgressive, very against ... I had found my character, my actor, but also my actor had made me understand the character — a kind of feeling of great humanity, but with something dangerous in there too.

In *Stealing Beauty*, I thought that I could identify more with Donal than with anybody else in the film. I know exactly why. It was great when he had to draw the girl in a scene. He could draw very well — it's not something every actor can do. It was then I found out that he had been doing it all his life. Donal was very discreet and had a fantastic way of not intruding. And so it was possible to film the chalk on the page, as I could see from the movement of his hand that he was a real artist. And of course a criminal!

Bernardo Bertolucci is a film maker.

11

Eugene Brady

Among Giants

When I first tried to write about Donal for this book I found I was doing it for selfish reasons. Donal worked with giants. Any one of them is more qualified to write about him than I am.

I will only say I was very lucky, honoured and privileged to collaborate with Donal McCann on *The Nephew*, my first picture.

Eugene Brady is a film director.

Gabriel Byrne

Celebration of Humanity

From *The Sunday Times*, July 25, 1999

It was the summer of 1983. The loveliest for years, people said. A summer of sun and light over the green and golden fields of Blarney in Co Cork. The sky-blue days seemed endless. We were filming John Banville's book *The Newton Letter* for Channel 4. I was playing a deluded historian; Donal McCann, ironically, a man dying of cancer.

He slouched into Jury's Hotel, cap pulled low to shadow the eyes, stomach thrust out like a docker, hands buried in too-large jeans, a racing page underarm. No handshake, just a jerk of the head, the perfunctory acknowledgement of my presence. 'Are you in this effing pantomime,' he said out of the corner of his mouth. I decided I did not like him. There seemed an arrogance about him, a contrived orneriness, a sham cool. I sensed a hidden and volcanic anger and the air about him seemed to shiver with menace. You wouldn't cross him. A look like a whip-crack was enough to instantly repel an uninvited intimacy or the palaver of everyday politeness.

He came, of course, dragging the mantle of greatness heedlessly behind him. His theatre performances were the stuff of legend, inspiring awe among audiences and peers alike. I had first seen him in the 1970s in *The Pallisers* on the BBC.

Sophisticated, sensitive, charismatic, sexual. And with an Irish accent. This at a time when in Britain most Irish actors were relegated to stereotypes — third rough fellow, drunk or priest. But McCann shone out with greatness and, like all real actors, transcended his nationality.

Later I saw him on stage, marvelling at the sincerity and naturalness of his playing. While others about him struck poses or were craven in their need to be loved by the audience, McCann seemed incapable of untruth or artifice. He was the George Best of the Abbey. He made it look so easy and yet what he achieved was so profoundly complex and courageous. He became the truest of actors, not by becoming somebody else (which many people believe acting to be) but by fearlessly revealing his own self. A man who held the dark mirror of truth up to his soul and fearlessly, shamelessly allowed us to examine it.

Yet that morning in Cork he seemed a restless, unfriendly creature, suspicious eye averted to some point in the distance. My heart sank at the prospect of spending the ensuing weeks working with him. But in truth I was, like most of us, afraid of him, awed by him and envious of his God-given gifts. What he thought of me I still have no idea.

It took days for the air between us to thaw and it happened most unexpectedly. I had just bought myself an antique car and one day impulsively offered to drive him to location. To my utter dismay he accepted. He walked around the motor, his body bending in the shininess of it. 'You didn't buy this yoke, did you?' he said with curl of a lip that passed for a smile, and I laughed. And so we came to know each other on those mornings driving to Blarney. We spoke about things important and trivial, the bulk of him beside me smoking, the beginning of grudging affection leaking out of him.

The mask sometimes removed, I came to know the shyness, the humour, the fierce intelligence, the unspoken pain that seemed fathomless, the passion for the gee-gees. Once he lay across the back seat, a newspaper across his face, tormented in hangover. He told me he felt like Foinavon, a horse that had won the National at 100/1 when all others had fallen at Bechers Brook. And once in a primitive joy he put his arm around me in whooping parody of the famous line from Frankenstein, as he roared: 'We're aloive!' I felt a childish thrill of acceptance in that strange, intimate moment.

At night he was gone, to the dogs, the pub, wherever, always alone, like Steppenwolf, for that was his way. It added to his mystery, the enigma of Donal.

One night I passed a bar and saw him standing there, pint in hand among the locals, watching a football match. So Donal, as the Americans would say.

Another image (prophetic it seems now) I cannot lose: Donal's character, already dying, standing by a fallen tree, a great oak, in a field at sunset. It was the final scene we filmed together and when it was completed he disappeared like a ghost.

The last performance I saw him give was Captain Boyle in *Juno and the Paycock*. 'The definitive Captain,' they said. 'The definitive Donal,' I say. All the humour, pain and compassion of his own life poured into O'Casey's great creation of tragedy and comedy. I saw him briefly afterwards. No reference to the play, to himself. The job was Oxo. 'How is it going, yourself?' The shy man's true revenge … a transcendent performance that haunts the memory. But the great triumph of his later life was a private one.

Alcoholism for years had brought him sorrow, loneliness and isolation. A cunning and powerful disease that he had arrested on a daily basis, ironically resulting in the real spiritual awakening that lit his later years.

We lost touch. I thought of him often, tried to buy one of his cartoons in an exhibition in Grogan's, and inquired of him to others. He's gone now and I regret we didn't meet again, because he was a rare one. Few people I know live their lives so privately and with such little regard for the approval of others. Neither fame nor fortune impressed him. Acting was a job. In these days when celebrity has become the new religion. Donal was the antithesis of a star.

That summer, he seemed touched by a golden rod. Sometimes I felt he would live forever, slouching haunted and graced among us, lighting up our path with the beauty of his restless soul. But the blinds are down now, Joxer, and the stage is silent, and we who were privileged to have known him have only the memory of him. And for that we are blessed.

Gabriel Byrne is an actor.

Des Cave

Slán Abhaile

Donal and myself share the month of May for our birthdays: his early, mine May 29th.

I first met Donal in the autumn of 1962. We were both enrolled at the National Academy for Theatre and Applied Arts in Camden Street. We spent two terms there. Our tutors were Abbey actor Bill Foley and Ray MacAnally, the Academy's principal.

In the summer of 1963 we both applied for and were accepted into the newly formed Abbey School of Acting, under Frank Dermody. The school also included Stephen Rea, Clive Geraghty, Máire O'Neill and Geraldine Plunkett, among others. We became members of the company some months later.

As new young Turks at the Abbey, we shared a rivalry that was both professional and social. Our theatrical godparents in the company were Philip O'Flynn and his wife Angela Newman who gave Donal and myself the nicknames of Biff and Baff (I cannot recall which was which!). We had great adventures both on and off stage in those early years.

Every summer during the Abbey's annual June break we were encouraged by the managing director, Ernest Blythe, to go west to the Connemara Gaeltacht to improve our spoken Irish skills, the train fare to Galway and one week's subsistence having been provided! But we never got further into the Gaelic heartland than the village of An Spidéal, the main reason being it was still within striking distance of the fleshpots of Galway City and the 'craic'.

We would borrow two bicycles from members of the Garda Síochána who were staying in the same digs as ourselves and away with us to O'Connor's in Salthill, all of fourteen or so miles. Returning in the early hours just in time to see the sun come up on Galway Bay. Saddle-sore but content.

I especially remember one really glorious sunny afternoon we were sitting on the rocks at the back of the harbour in Spiddal. I was preparing to go for a swim. It was so warm and the sea so inviting that Donal expressed a wish to do likewise. Being a non-swimmer, though, was somewhat of a drawback for him. I suggested I could start him off on the rudiments of learning to swim. He asked if that would require the removal of all underwear, with special emphasis on his long-sleeved woollen vest (which he wore winter and summer!). When I replied that it would, thus endeth the first and only lesson!

Donal left the Abbey in the early Seventies. We met theatrically on a number of occasions afterwards when he guested with the company but socially, unfortunately, we saw less and less of each other except for telephone conversations, punctuated by long, meaningful pauses which usually concluded with Donal saying, 'We must do this more often. I enjoy these little chats'! I would gladly swap some of today's buzz and chatter for one of those long meaningful pauses.

Dónal, a chara, slán abhaile.

Abbey Theatre
May 2000

Des Cave is an actor.

Sinéad Cusack

In Conversation with Faith O'Grady

I first met Donal when I was sixteen, with my father and his uncle, Fr Leo McCann. I was at a very impressionable age, and I just thought he was extraordinarily witty and amusing company. I didn't know about his talent then but I was very taken with him. He was three years older than I was, and very easy to talk to. There were periods in our lives when he was incredibly difficult to communicate with because he was going through such hell in his life. At the time of our first meeting, however, he was wonderfully forthcoming. I went to see him subsequently at the Queen's Theatre and when I saw him walk on stage — I don't exaggerate at all — it seemed to me as if all the light in the theatre had concentrated on him. He seemed to draw the attention of the audience in an extraordinary way into his character and what he was doing. He had an ability to make an audience just focus on him completely. I think it was his fantastic concentration and complete habitation of the character he was playing. We didn't become friends until I joined the Abbey myself and then we became close. We were in and out of each other's lives pretty well until he died. There were long periods of time when I didn't see him and he might drop me a quick line with a drawing or a poem. He was a wonderfully witty correspondent when he did write, which wasn't often. His letters always made me laugh.

Donal was a very disturbing presence. When I say that I'm not denigrating him; I'm saying that he made you re-evaluate, he made you re-think. He had such a strange and quirky mind. It is very difficult for me to describe the quality he had on stage and the quality he had in life, except to say it was disturbing, it was dangerous. You never knew where you were. He could go from extraordinary sweetness to vile temper. You simply did not know where you were, but throughout all the years I always knew that Donal would be on my side in a scrap and I would be on his. At times he was incredibly curmudgeonly and difficult. But I always enjoyed his company.

We worked together a lot over the years. The ones that stand out are *The Playboy of the Western World* for the BBC, with him playing Seánín Keogh and me playing Peigín, and *The Shadow of a Gunman* in which he played Seumas Shields and I played Minnie. That was for the BBC also, but before that we played the prince and the princess in the Abbey pantomime *as Gaeilge*. Usually, they would bring in a singing prince and princess for this event but when Donal and I played the parts they decided to have an acting pair — we might have been reasonable in the acting area, but neither of us could really carry a tune — so they cast Donal as the *prionsa* and me as the *banphrionsa*.

But we did have to do some singing, such as the Beatles' song 'Yesterday', *as Gaeilge*. I was out of tune. Donal had to pick up from me. So I would drop a couple of notes, then he would drop a couple more notes. It was like Chinese whispers and by the time we got to the end of the song we were totally out of tune.

Then there was *Faith Healer* on stage and that wa[s] extraordinary experience for me. To start off just to wa[tch] him. It was that concentration he had and that element [of] danger and damage. It made you want to find out what was going on in that character's head.

I think he found peace in the last years. I think it was to do with giving up the drink. Also — I hesitate to talk about it — but I think he found a faith that he had never had before. He had a very personal relationship with God. When he talked about God it was as if he was talking about the bloke next door whom he knew extremely well. It was an intimate relationship.

I saw a lot of him when we were filming *Stealing Beauty* in Tuscany for two months. I have to say that Bertolucci was in awe of his talent. I had suggested to Bernardo that he go and see Donal in *The Steward of Christendom* because he was looking for someone to play my husband in the film. He cast him the following day, I think. He was bowled over by what he saw on stage as were most of the audience. Working with him again was very inspiring but, as in his personal life, he had a disturbing presence which sometimes made it difficult. He was a perfectionist. His rhythms as an actor were so unpredictable that at times it was hard to work with him, but most of the time I loved it.

I subsequently did *The Nephew* with him, and that was the last time we worked together. He was in great form then, a happy man and an incredibly funny companion. He was such an astonishing actor and, as I say, an amusing companion because he came from left field. He was very unusual and he led you places you never expected. His comments were always delivered out of the side of his mouth in a mumble.

think he rediscovered life after the drink. He went through the hellish years struggling with it. When he came through, it was like coming into the light. Once he made the decision it seems that (maybe he hid the cost) he never went back. He never preached and he continued to love pub life.

Life was never easy for Donal. He had some real devils which he had to fight. That's another reason why he was such a great actor, because those devils which plagued him in his life actually fuelled his art. He had to fight quite a hard fight and it sometimes made him difficult, but there was always a sweetness and a compassion inherent in his nature. He was incredibly generous and gave away a lot of money. He didn't save for his future.

He was very upbeat about getting sick. One will never know the fears and panic that were in him those last years, because he was a private man. All I could see was that he refused to give in. I saw him about three months before he died but I didn't see him in those last bad days.

There is no actor on the face of the planet who is happy with the body of his work, but he must have known the high regard in which he was held and I think that retrospective in Galway really, really pleased him [*It Must Be Done Right*, the Bob Quinn documentary on Donal McCann produced in 1999]. It was just magnificent. You see evidence there of the humour I'm talking about. And he was so clever and interesting in his thinking. He was never led by schools of thought. He had his own.

Sinéad Cusack is an actor.

Lelia Doolan

Dónal Óg

A friend wrote in a letter to me:

*I am not much good for anything today. I am so saddened
by the shortness of Donal's life.*

And that got me to thinking of you, Donal, and the parts of
your life that crossed into mine. We never worked together
even though we met here and there: after the play; in a pub, in
someone's house.

Fleeting conversations, never sure which one of you was
really there. I often enjoyed your face-rubbing ironies, your
wry reflections; sometimes I was wary of your taciturn
moroseness. Invariably, there was a fair amount of silence.
None of those details matter much.

What matters is that you took yourself seriously as a
worker in the arts — eventually — some might say. There was
plenty of self-deprecation and the modest shrugging-off
required by our bourgeois niceties, offset, however, by the
depressing, nagging doubt: what is it all for? Somewhere in
the dark intensity of *Faith Healer* that doubt must have been
resoundingly resolved: I am the crossroads at which things
happen.

The most dangerous and potentially fruitful time of work in
the theatre is during rehearsal when actors experiment and
invent, probe experience and the text for the moment of light,

of insight, of balance with one another. Again and again, these moments are reached and discarded as the actors transform themselves into a new combination of forces, delving into hidden caverns of emotion and experience. Donal was a veteran of such absorbing and addictive expeditions; not from mere recklessness but from the true passion of an explorer testing himself against elemental gods. Auden defined the tortuous path:

> From bad lands, where eggs are small and dear,
> Climbing to worse by a stonier
> Track when all are spent, we hear it – the right song
> For the wrong time of year

It is not always good weather for the arts, especially when affluence, in its noisy ignorance, attempts to colonise everything. In such times it is healing to find opinionated and convincing evidence that one man's work can insinuate a real tune into the cacophony. A galaxy of real tunes.

At another point on the compass, there was Captain Molineux in *The Shaughraun*, a lisping ass of a chap, all fancy gestures and boiling airs. If, as a Frenchman said, 'the body is a grouping of lived-through meanings that moves towards its equilibrium', *this* was equilibrium.

So I salute and revere you, Donal: troubled, workaday, Dublin genius — and the sweetness, at last, of your vulnerable mortality. A man's life is not measured in the shortness of his days but in the many days his art ennobled.

Lelia Doolan is a former Artistic Director of the Abbey Theatre.

Joe Dowling

The Blessing of a Great Talent

By its very nature, theatrical performance can only survive in the human memory. The immediacy and the energy of the moment are lost as soon as it is realised and even the most vivid portrayals fade with the passage of time. In a lifetime of theatre-going, only a handful of performances stand out in my memory with clarity. Micheál MacLiammóir as Oscar Wilde, Cyril Cusack and Siobhán McKenna in *The Cherry Orchard* and Niall Toibin in *Borstal Boy* are all examples of memorable performances that have withstood the inevitable destruction of grey cells.

It is a measure of the greatness of Donal McCann that a number of his performances remain vivid and alive even after many years. The first sight I had of Donal's acting ability was in a now-forgotten play *The Call* by Tom Coffey at the Abbey Theatre in the early Sixties. Donal and Robert Carlile, a brilliant actor also lost before his time, played brothers, one a clerical student home on holidays and the other a bad egg who tried to persuade the saintly youth to abandon his vocation. (This *was* the early Sixties!) Bob Carlile was young, blond and fresh-faced as the seminarian. Donal was dark, brooding and clearly up to no good as the older brother. While the details of this melodramatic piece are long gone, the sense of McCann's presence and the promise it revealed are vividly recalled. It was clear that a new star had burst onto the Irish theatrical

25

scene who had the ability to transcend the material and create a full and rounded character from very little.

As time went on and the performances became more and more layered, Donal's talents deepened and became reflective of the complexity of his own life and personality. In *Tarry Flynn*, P.J. O'Connor's adaptation of Patrick Kavanagh's seminal novel of rural Ireland, Donal captured to perfection the longing and the frustration of the young poet dreaming of a better life away from his family's stony patch of a field in poverty-stricken Monaghan. In Dion Boucicault's *The Shaughraun*, he created a unique caricature of the hapless British officer who, stammer and all, found himself at the mercy of Irish cunning. His comic timing and innate charm awakened a London audience to his genius when the Abbey brought Hugh Hunt's production to the World Theatre Season in 1968. It was the beginning of an international career that drew McCann away from Irish theatre for some time. His roots were always in Ireland and while the possibility of fame and stardom was always a reality in his career, it was never the motivating factor in his decision about roles. His emphasis was always on the importance of the text and the quality of the writing. Even at times of lowest morale and setback, he would reject the easy option and remain out of work rather than engage with writing he did not admire.

What made McCann so special an actor? A talent for acting is a gift from the gods and cannot be explained in rational terms. Much as I advocate the training of vocal and physical skills in the actor, I believe strongly that acting cannot be taught. It is an instinct, a genetic predisposition and an itching need that some people have as a way of expressing themselves to the world. Off stage, actors are rarely demonstrative personalities and, indeed, many can be painfully shy. The few who display flamboyance and public temperament are greatly outnumbered by the many whose work onstage is their only statement to the world. The combination of personality and intelligence, of physique and instinct mixed together with an acute sensitivity to human behaviour are what makes a great performer.

Great talent is not always a blessing and can be the source of real insecurities and emotional trauma. In Donal's case, the introverted nature of his personality, a brooding and tortured imagination and a highly attuned sense of self combined to create a unique approach to every part he played. He had the ability to take a character imagined by the writer and without changing a word, make it sound and feel like his own creation. Lines sounded newly minted every time he spoke them and the originality of his interpretation often surprised even the author. He was gifted with a magnificent voice and a powerful physical presence. On stage or screen, he conveyed mystery and a sense of danger. The presence was overwhelming and the possibility always exciting. Rarely did he disappoint audiences and he was his own most exacting critic. Night after night, he would work diligently to ensure that a particular moment would resonate as he wished, and woe betide any actor or director who did not live up to his highest ideals of dedication and exploration.

Working with Donal as a director was challenging, instructive and, at times, maddening. He was highly intelligent and brought all his personal complexity into the room with him. Any idea from the director had to be thought out clearly and offered as suggestion rather than instruction. Invariably, he had thought about the scene even more than the director and was impatient of innovation that did not emerge naturally from the text. Working with him over many years, we developed a kind of shorthand and a mutual respect that allowed rehearsal to be creative and entertaining. But I was never fully at ease with him or him with me. Warily, we would circle one another with ideas and suggestions and I watched for the changes of mood that frequently overtook him. It was essential to ensure that his restless imagination was always occupied. In the early days, when drinking was an issue, there were tensions that often disrupted the flow of rehearsal and situations were created that might have been fatal to the project. However, we would both always pull back from the brink and an uneasy peace would be established.

Even in those difficult times, the creativity never stopped. He was full of ideas and courageous choices that illuminated every scene and each line. The suggestions would flow from him and I would watch in awe as he wrestled with a line or a scene. He never gave up until he was satisfied that he had an original way of doing it. As time went on and he bravely faced his dependence on alcohol, his energies were freed to become even more creative and inclusive of other ideas and people. The internal peace he found towards the end of his life did not rob him of his originality. The spirituality that replaced the demons was fuel to a new and even more profound exploration of his talents. Anyone who saw his masterly Lear-like Thomas Dunne in Sebastian Barry's *The Steward of Christendom* realised that his work had moved to an even greater plane and a whole new chapter opened up for him. It is a cruel irony that it was to be his last performance.

No matter who plays it in the future, for me, forever, Donal will be Frank Hardy, the eponymous faith healer of Brian Friel's masterpiece. It was a performance where character and actor became one as the evening wore on. The character, one of Friel's most complex figures, lives in a temporary and fickle world that every actor knows well. Travelling in an old battered van with his manager and wife (or mistress), offering his services as faith healer to the desperate souls in remote villages in Scotland and Wales, he lives with the constant fear that his gift or talent will desert him and that he will not be able to 'perform'. Weaving fantasies with fact, his monologues recount incidents from the strange journey that leads to his death. It was a perfect part for Donal McCann. It combined intelligence, sensitivity, spirituality, excessive behaviour and the awareness that talent cannot be trusted, that the performance doesn't always happen on demand. He understood it instinctively and, from the beginning of rehearsal, played it to perfection.

Working as director on that play with him over many years, it was inspiring to watch him grow into the role so completely. The last performance in London's Royal Court Theatre stands out in my memory as one of the greatest nights of theatre I have witnessed. As Frank Hardy made his way downstage for the final moment of epiphany, delicately removing an imaginary piece of fluff from his coat, certain that he was going to his death, the focus of the entire audience was on his every tiny gesture. The stillness in the theatre was a palpable demonstration of the collective experience that makes live theatre a unique event. In that moment, I understood the nature of his theatrical greatness. A complete concentration on the character, his ability to hold our attention fully and the magic within him to communicate his thoughts and feelings clearly to the audience, made it a moment to hold onto forever.

Among our many other collaborations, the Gate Theatre production of O'Casey's *Juno and the Paycock* in 1986 was probably the most famous and the most successful. It started as an idea I presented to Michael Colgan shortly after I left the

Abbey Theatre in 1985. I had long wanted to do the play with McCann. The complicated history we both had with the Abbey prevented it from being realised in the traditional home of O'Casey's work. Colgan has always been one to embrace a challenge and his enthusiastic leadership of the project made it happen. The casting of the other roles around McCann was a difficult task. I was determined that we should have a cast who had never played the parts before. I had been disappointed with an Abbey production I had directed in 1979 where the weight of tradition had stifled the play and denied it a fresh approach. With Geraldine Plunkett as Juno, John Kavanagh as Joxer Daly and the legendary Maureen Potter as Maisie Madigan, Michael Colgan and I knew we had a strong team to give the play a new look.

At the centre of all this, of course, was Donal McCann as Captain Boyle. It was a typically inspired reading of the role. I have always believed that the power of the play lies in the reality of poverty and deprivation masked by the civil-war horrors that Mrs Tancred's speech so movingly reveals. The real strength of O'Casey's portrait of Dublin life is the recognition that whatever the political issues, the real lives of the people will not change until social issues are addressed. Donal immediately embraced the ideas and took them further than I could ever have hoped. His performance dominated the play.

The success of that production took us to Edinburgh, Jerusalem and finally in 1988, to Broadway. Its acclaim by the New York critics led to the expectation that it would stay there for a season. A mythology has been created that Donal refused to play for longer than the allotted time, thus denying the production chances for awards and so forth. In fact, the show had been brought to New York as part of a festival and the terms of our visas dictated the length of run. Donal was indeed reluctant to extend his contract but so were others in the cast who had both professional and personal obligations in Dublin. Such was the power of McCann's personality that it was assumed that his voice was the deciding factor.

He played the part for two years and then decided that enough was enough. No matter what blandishments were placed before him, once he had made his mind up to quit a part, nothing could persuade him. That was one of his most compelling features as an artist and as a person. It was a measure of both the seriousness of the man and the integrity of the artist that McCann never allowed any kind of fame and celebrity to overwhelm him or to impress him. He wrestled with many demons, and he was only at ease with himself towards the end of his life. However, he had a profound sense of who he was as an artist. He knew how good he was and did not need the acclaim of critics or the phoney celebration of stardom to confirm it. He was not afraid to say no to work he did not admire and he knew instinctively when he had achieved something special in a performance.

A year after his death, it still feels unreal and temporary. I still expect the call at any hour of the day or night offering a range of ideas, a torrent of humour and the odd scabrous story. Even during his final illness, he never lost that spirit that made him so special to all who knew him. In one conversation towards the end, I asked him if he thought he would ever go on stage again. 'The very word "stage-door" fills me with terror' was his reply. I have a feeling that was true of his whole career. He was an actor who needed to act but who did not always relish the consequences of exposing so much of himself through his performances. He was an artist who was always truthful in his work and that took a heavy emotional toll on him. The audiences benefited greatly from his honesty and those of us who were privileged to be a part of his life and work know that we have seen greatness and witnessed a unique talent. The stage performances are gone and only a handful of films capture the real quality. But human memory will keep him alive for many years to come.

Joe Dowling is Artistic Director of the Guthrie Theater, Minneapolis.

Drawing by Donal of himself as Captain Boyle and John Kavanagh as Joxer, from *Juno and the Paycock* by Sean O'Casey.

Paul Durcan

From *Christmas Day*

XIII

I was in Meath when you phoned at 8.30 a.m.:
'Paul, will you meet me in Dublin at 10.45
Outside the Carmelite Church in Beaumont –
Around the corner from Beaumont Hospital?'

In the early morning fog I drove across country,
The hills of East Meath and North Dublin,
By way of the Bolies and Stamullen,
The Naul and the Bog of the Ring.

Although I tried to guess why you had phoned
– Had you been sentenced to death by a doctor?
– Had you decided to marry or to become a monk?
– Had you decided to resign?

I did not pry, being grateful to you
For waking me, for being the cause
Of my driving along empty roads
In the heat haze of a May morning.

Crossroads after empty crossroads.
No signposts. No traffic signs.
Queen Anne's Lace, furze, white
Blossom of blackthorn in fog.

I could not see the tops of the hills
Of Bellewstown and Fourknocks.
I'd slept badly but now I felt well.
Filling up with the right kind of emptiness.

I hoped I'd be able to find the church in time.
I knew where Beaumont Hospital was –
Having been visiting Colm Tóibín at Christmas:
His circles of friends feasting at his well.

Buckets of time! I pulled in to the large
Carpark of the Church of the Nativity of Our Lord
At 10.40 and as I scanned the other parked cars
I saw you stand up the far side of the carpark.

You circled round my car. Leaning up against it,
Your hands on the roof over the passenger door,
You said: 'I've decided to put my head under the water.
I want to get baptized – rightly this time.'

I stare down at the ground – pebbles, grass
And – one solitary marigold
Wearing its heart on its tongue – its wet, orange tongue.
I mutter: 'Good man yourself.'

I glance up at you –
Odd man out.
I kick a pebble, staring at the one solitary marigold.
Jesus Christ!

You say that friends have chided you
For your habit of saying 'God bless.'
Henceforth you will be able to say with authority
'God bless'.

You are edgy before the ceremony at eleven.
You whisper: 'I want to pee.' I point out a tree
At a discreet distance from the adjacent primary school.
You step off into the trees at the far end of the church.

The priest comes out a door, shakes hands, smiles:
'Let's be about our business.'
We sit in a tiny oratory with five sanctuary lamps.
He puts on a white stole over pullover and slacks.

The priest hands me his copy of the Jerusalem Bible.
In my trembling witness's 'speaking-in-public voice'
I read from the Gospel of St John, Chapter 3:
The Conversation with Nicodemus.

'Not to judge the world
But so that through him the world might be saved.
No one who believes in him will be judged;
But whosoever does not believe is judged already.'

Words that scandalize.
I discover that conscience is the courage to improvise.
When the priest asks you to repeat 'Holy Catholic Church'
You change it to 'Holy Catholic *Christian* Church'.

Driving back to Drogheda – to the Tropical Medicine Unit
Of Our Lady of Lourdes Hospital –
I am to be vaccinated against Yellow Fever
Before my tour of Brazil –

I stop at the Ivory Coast pub in Balbriggan
For a bottle of mineral water.
I glimpse your sockets pop open beneath your bowed skull
Casting a warm eye on death.

Late last night reading the racing pages
You saw that in the 2.45 at Nottingham today
Christian Flight is 20 to 1.
Your life is a form of risk. What do you do?

If you were to go through with your baptism and back
   Christian Flight
She would not win!
So what you had to do is go through with your baptism
And not back Christian Flight!

'CHRISTIAN FLIGHT SURPRISES' is the headline
In next day's newspaper.
Your dedication to chance as the ethic of fate;
Self-denial, humility, intuition.

'Christian Flight completed a rags-to-riches story
With a success in the Bradmore Fillies' Handicap at
   Nottingham yesterday.
The six-year-old battled to a neck victory
Over Le Bal at odds of 20 to 1.'

Paul Durcan is a poet.

John Fogarty and Chris Rourke
of Fogarty's Bookmakers

In Conversation with Faith O'Grady

Chris Rourke: Donal came into Fogarty's for the first time in 1990. He used to drop in once every so often. I think he liked coming up and seeing our business. He'd sit down and have a cup of coffee. He loved to have a bit of a chat. I think he'd get bored when he wasn't reading scripts, so he'd be reading form instead.

John Fogarty: He had no regard for money. He wasn't a compulsive gambler though. He just liked all kinds of betting. He didn't care about the stakes and wasn't a big punter. He'd ring up from America to bet on the Breeder's Cup or the Superbowl. He'd say about New York, 'It's a quiet village — no bookies and the shooting's ended for the day.' He'd talk mainly about betting and the horses, not about his acting work or the actors he would have met. Apparently he did the Ballygowan ad in the back of a taxi. He paid his account with that cheque. He liked to see the ad because then he knew there would be more money on the way. When asked why he hadn't been in the film *Far and Away*, he replied that the script was shite and that he wasn't able to ride horses.

CR: He was very down to earth, very Dublin with a real dry wit. You'd meet him on the street and you'd say 'How's your luck' and he'd say, 'Poxy'.

JF: He was very kind to my father who was also a bookie and asked my parents to a Lord Mayor's award ceremony. He had sympathy for us bookies unlike most of the punters who come in.

CR: Actually, I think he would have loved to have been a bookmaker. He would talk for hours about horses and was very knowledgeable. He didn't bet for the money but just for enjoyment.

JF: I went to see him after his first operation and he said when he saw me that he would be paying his account. I said that wasn't the reason for my visit at all and handed him a present of a block of cheese. At that he said, 'You can go now!' All part of his dry wit.

John Fogarty is a bookmaker.
Chris Rourke is a bookie at Fogarty's.

Joseph Hurley

Wham Bang

From *Irish Echo*, January 29-February 4, 1997

Sebastian Barry's *The Steward of Christendom* arrived at the Brooklyn Academy of Music's Majestic Theater last week, preceded by the kind of anticipatory excitement, both for the play and for the performance being given by Donal McCann in the gruelling title role, that, in most instances, is almost guaranteed to dim the lustre of any venture.

Rest assured, Barry's play, the fifth in a projected series of seven dramas based on his own Dublin family, is just as rare and beautiful a work as we've been hearing and reading for the last two years, as the production moved from London to Dublin and then to Australia and New Zealand. Factor in the accessibility and daring of the play's poetic intensity, and the impact of Barry's achievement may seem even greater than the advance word indicated.

As for McCann's work as Thomas Dunne, a character based on the playwright's great-grandfather, James Dunne, a highly placed inspector of the Dublin Metropolitan Police during the difficult first quarter of the century, the actor has clearly earned a place in the rare atmosphere occupied by such legendary performances as Laurence Olivier's Oedipus,

Laurette Taylor's Amanda in *The Glass Menagerie*, and Lee J. Cobb's Willy Loman in *Death of a Salesman*.

The measure of McCann's wondrous discipline and flawless taste may be found in the fact that the star, given one of the longest and meatiest roles since Lear, never once allows himself one of those semaphoring 'big moments' by which even the finest actors, most of them anyway, remind their audiences of their greatness.

It might be possible to witness this performance and be moved and impressed, without quite fully realizing its incredible complexity, subtlety, and difficulty, not to mention the toll it takes on the actor involved, even playing it just six times a week, as is the case at the Majestic, where Barry's astonishing diamond of a play will be in residence.

The rough parallels between *The Steward of Christendom* and *King Lear* are perhaps unavoidable, since here, as in Shakespeare, is a once-powerful man, father of three extremely diverse daughters, nearing the end of his life, edging in and out of abject madness and trying to come to terms with events and circumstances almost entirely beyond his understanding.

While Lear has a kingdom to divide, Thomas Dunne has nothing to 'distribute' but the breadth of his experience and the richness of his memories, most of them tinged with sorrow, regret and incompleteness. Nevertheless, the shadows of Lear and even August Strindberg's *The Father* cross and recross the scenes of Barry's wonderful play like the images of eagles soaring above a snowy mountain range.

The mere word 'poetry' can deal a grievous wound to a theatrical venture, but it must nevertheless be said that Barry's writing is filled with the sort of casually beautiful imagery and lyricism that characterizes the very best work of Tennessee Williams, frequently referred to as the most poetically gifted of American writers for the theater in our time.

Free-standing fragments and isolated images from *Steward* are very likely to follow you out of the theater and haunt you for days and weeks after the last light has dimmed on designer Julian McGowan's striking evocation, the drab room in the county home in Baltinglass, Co Wicklow, to which Dunne is confined in his madness.

One of the luminous graces of Barry's superb writing is the ordinariness and accessibility of its imagery, much of it as easy to enfold as the rural references to be found in the poetry of Seamus Heaney. Tales involving dogs, horses, lambs, chickens, and ducks abound in Dunne's staggering journey into his own past, while a strong sense of the Irish earth, the very soil on which Barry's restless characters walk and live seems almost to leach up through the battered planks of the chamber that has become the old policeman's 'kingdom'.

The magic of *Steward* is rendered with enhanced power and specificity by Johanna Towns's inspired lighting, which, as it helps ease the play from its 1932 'present tense' toward its numerous and eloquent flashbacks to 1922, imbues McGowan's set with echoes of the lithographs and etchings of Edward Munch.

Dunne, in his seventies in the county home, was roughly forty or so when Queen Victoria died in 1901, by which time he had lived through the first half of his professional career in law enforcement, and, as he puts it, 'risen as high as a Catholic could' in the Dublin Metropolitan Police at Dublin Castle in the city he loved, understood and knew, street-by-street and lane-by-lane, in those vanquished pre-republican days.

The old man, haunted by memories of his three daughters and perhaps most searingly by thoughts of his only son too short of stature to serve in the DMP, but fully tall enough to be killed in France, fighting for the English in World War I, roils and rages through the tattered fabric of the disordered, disintegrating mind, bringing everything back as if drenched in etcher's acid.

Two functionaries of the county home, an attendant and a matron, are played movingly and well by, respectively, Kieran Ahern and Maggie McCarthy, the latter in particular supplying the only warmth and human kindness the failing giant, now made obsolete by circumstances, will experience in his final, fading days, providing him with a suit held together with yellow thread substituting for the gold braid of his long-remembered professional uniforms.

As the daughters, the neurasthenic Maud, the loyal physically impaired Annie, and the youngest and most beloved Dolly, Ali White, Tina Kellegher (familiar here for her work in Stephen Frears's popular film version of Roddy Doyle's *The Snapper*) and Aislin McGuckin offer strong support, as do Rory Murray, doubling as Dunne's painter son-in-law, Matt, and unnamed, briefly seen Recruit, and the child actor Carl Brennan in the wordless role of Willie, the old man's only son, buried in a foreign field.

But support it definitely is and should be, since Thomas Dunne is the engine of Sebastian Barry's obsession, and as fleshed out by the redoubtable Donal McCann, dominates a compelling endeavour without ever, for even a moment, converting it to a one-actor event or the glittering star turn it could easily have become in other hands.

Barry's stories and speeches, some of them running to two and three pages in the printed text, are so brilliantly cradled by McCann's extraordinary vocal instrument, with its hints of roughness and its traces of purest Dublin intonation, that they come across more as intimately rendered stream of consciousness, a jumbled tangle of thoughts and feelings, than as the arduous monologues they actually are.

Max Stafford-Clark, the much-honoured artist director of London's Royal Court Theatre, is to be commended for the tight, no-nonsense control he has maintained on the play, and perhaps especially for the wisdom and foresight that motivated him to commission the work in the first place.

There is great work here, and the very light and air of the city somehow seem clearer and purer for the temporary presence of *The Steward of Christendom* at Brooklyn's Majestic. Walk if you must, but go.

Joseph Hurley is a theatre critic.

Neil Jordan

Out On His Own

I had cast Donal in *Angel* in a part that needed a kind of monosyllabic anti-acting and he didn't seem to have enjoyed the experience. At the time I think he seemed to regard movies as a second and inferior cousin to the theatre. Three years and two movies later I was in a Dublin pub and saw him drinking with Louis Stewart. Two Dublin men of a hard kind of genius and, when drunk, a biting, generally scabrous wit.

'Why the fuck did you never put me in any more of your movies?' he muttered. 'Because you didn't seem to enjoy the first one,' I said. 'Enjoyment has nothing to do with it,' he replied.

To change the subject Mr Stewart began a story of a trumpeter who had his teeth taken out, and had sets of falsers made based on the embouchures of the great trumpet players. So to play in the style of Dizzy Gillespie, he'd insert the Dizzy Gillespie set and give the trumpet a blow, and so on.

I think I was that naïve that I believed him. I was also naïve enough to believe Donal and I cast him in *High Spirits*, a film that would turn out to be a Hollywood experience, and not a good one. I must have been aware that something was going wrong with the movie at the top — the level of the international stars — because I spent most of my time and took most of my pleasure working with the character actors, improvising elaborate pieces of business. With Donal this process could go on forever, since he could actually create something out of nothing. We had a small, moustachioed American producer who saw his job as something between Torquemada and Inspector Clousseau and we took elaborate and quite sadistic pleasure in inventing scenes, pieces of dialogue, whole subplots, behind his back. The most comical thing about the whole process in the end was the reams of footage that the studio left on the cutting-room floor. After the film came out and was inevitably savaged, *The New Yorker* film critic Pauline Kael rang me up and asked could she see my original cut. I explained that it didn't exist, since I was not allowed to get to the stage of watching a full assembly. So I spent a weekend in the Hollywood house I was living in at the time and looked through piles of videos of the footage we had shot. There was Donal, in scene after scene, displaying an understated wit that had been cut from the loud, noisy piece of work that was playing in the cinemas. I returned to Dublin determined to reassemble the film and got an editor, Pat Duffner, to agree to do it. He went to Shepperton to get his hands on the footage but was not allowed, because Shepperton hadn't been paid. Which just goes to show you can't beat the system.

I managed to preserve his performance in *The Miracle*, in a part I had written for him. It was the part of a musician, and an alcoholic one at that. Donal at the time was waging a kind of war with alcohol, which I think had reached a stalemate. His tactics in that war were ingenious, utterly original, and without any point whatsoever. He would go on the dry for the length of a performance. The minute that performance wrapped he'd go off the wagon. So, after I'd said, 'That's a wrap', that happiest of human beings, that actor of genius with whom I'd been

45

working for six weeks, sat in the bar of the Bray Head Hotel and ordered a pint of Guinness. The minute the froth touched his lips, a cloud came over his features, as if the moon had blocked the sun. The transformation was extraordinary, all the more apparent, perhaps, because of the actor he was.

I saw him next in *The Steward of Christendom*, a play that I cannot imagine without him. Sitting in the theatre, feeling the almost sacral nature of his relationship with the audience, I began to see elements in his performance that no movie I had seen him in, certainly none of mine, had ever caught. He could change the moment in so many ways, there was an existential quality to the meaning of his performance that in an odd way needed the transitory nature of a theatrical event. What was happening on stage would never happen again, in quite the same way. He had reached a far happier place in himself, I realised when I met him backstage. Whatever that place was I didn't want to question. But I did want him to be in *Michael Collins*. He shook his head gently and told me Bertolucci had him first.

I saw the Bertolucci film when it came out and thought with a kind of niggardly pleasure that Bertolucci hadn't captured him either. And I began to fret about the reasons the camera couldn't nail the subtlety, the immediacy, I had seen so many times on stage. My first memory was of him and Peter O'Toole in *Godot*, at the Abbey during the Seventies, in the kind of sublime double-act, and double-acting, that Beckett and O'Casey engender in great performers. It was a double-act that he repeated, with John Kavanagh in *Juno*, more than a decade later. Some actors, out of psychological or pathological compulsion, suck all the air out of the space around them. With Donal's intelligence and subtlety, this was never the case. He fed off other actors, gave as much energy as he took. Yet he was alone on stage for two of his greatest performances — in *Faith Healer* and *The Steward of Christendom*. But watching him, alone and naked — literally so, in the latter play — you realised he still had a partner, there was still a collaboration, a double-act going on. That partner, of course, was the audience.

Neil Jordan is a film maker.

John Kavanagh

In Conversation with Faith O'Grady

I first saw Donal in the 1960s in the Queen's Theatre pantomime, and immediately became a great admirer of his. I think I saw him about twenty times in *The Shaughraun* in the new Abbey but never would have told him that as he would have been embarrassed.

Over the years we acted together from time to time, but got to know each other (as well as one could with Donal, anyway) on the *Juno and the Paycock* tour in 1986 and 1987. We toured Dublin, Edinburgh, Jerusalem and Broadway, and during that time we always shared a dressing room.

His conversation was staccato, monosyllabic and he certainly didn't suffer fools gladly. On one occasion, an Irish journalist who had been trying to find negative things to write about our tour came to have a chat with us. Donal, having fabricated a yarn, proceeded to explain to the journalist that he had been up the Mount of Olives on a camel and that he was having terrible trouble with his performance because a camel hair had become lodged in his nostril. Sure enough, the story was headlined in a prominent Irish paper the next day.

I also remember a time in New York during the same tour when Katharine Hepburn came to our dressing room after the show, full of admiration, and said to us, 'How do you people do it?' and Donal's reply was, 'From watching you, Madam'.

I know that Donal was re-baptised in his later years, but he had always been a spiritual person. Before every performance we would nominate someone who had passed away or who was suffering in some way, and we would dedicate the performance to them. The stage became a sacred place.

He was very concerned with other people's well-being, and was a deeply kind man, always giving unusual, unexpected presents. He was also very helpful to members of the cast if you wanted some advice on the text.

I remember just after *The Dead* had been completed someone coming up to Donal in the pub and saying, 'I believe John Huston said you are one of the best actors he has ever worked with. How does that feel?' and Donal replied, 'It's a terrible responsibility'.

His stage presence, clarity of diction and thought, and his absolute commitment to storytelling was a real inspiration. His loss is immeasurable.

John Kavanagh is an actor.

Line drawing on an envelope, featuring Donal as Captain Boyle and John Kavanagh as Joxer, on tour with *Juno* in Jerusalem.

David Kelly

Abiding Memories

Some years ago Peter O'Toole sent me a wonderful screenplay of Sean O'Casey's *Juno and the Paycock*. He wanted me to play Joxer Daly in a film version, which would star Donal McCann and the splendid Vanessa Redgrave, known affectionately, due to her stature, as Big Van. I was of course thrilled, and in Donal's company burst into verse:

Peter O'Toole, a darlin' man
Has the backing and the plan
To film Juno and the P
Peter O'Toole
Big Van
Donal McCann
And ME!!

'That's a desperate poem,' said McCann. He always had taste. Sadly the project never happened.

We were friends, and there are memories of certain performances that will stay in my mind for the rest of my days, but I have another memory of Donal that means more to me than I can say.

I loved my father dearly, and when he died in 1980 a small group of neighbours and a few actor friends, such as Aiden

Grennell and Iris Lawlor, gathered at the church to receive his remains and again at the funeral the following day. Donal was there. When my mother died only five weeks later, again Donal graced the occasion with his presence at both the removal and the funeral.

That is of immense importance to me and is an abiding memory of his sensitivity and kindness.

David Kelly is an actor.

Eamon Kelly

Who Won the War?

A history of the Great War was being shown on television in
The Flowing Tide. Two old-timers with ringside seats were
deeply engrossed in the affair. Donal McCann and I were
sitting near them having a drink, after the curtain had come
down on Tom Murphy's *A Crucial Week in the Life of a
Grocer's Assistant* at the Abbey. It was the first time we had
been in a play together. We'd had a row earlier in the run. I
had taken umbrage at something Donal had said, and went for
him in no uncertain fashion. He'd been surprised at my display
of temper, but we'd made it up, and remained firm friends for
as long as I knew him.

The guns exploded on the small screen. New sounds added
to old film footage. The soldiers moved with the jerky
movements everyone appeared to have in those early movies.
Donal was fascinated by the two old men and the interest they
showed in the action. They were goggle-eyed looking at the
screen. We tried to determine where their sympathies lay, and
from a few grunts of satisfaction after a British bayonet charge
was repelled, we decided they were pro-German.

It was near closing time. In fact Donal and I felt on our way
from the theatre that our stay in the bar would be short. Just
the one. Sure enough, only minutes had elapsed when Danny,
the barman, called 'Time gentlemen please!', and with a total

lack of ceremony he reached for the television button and turned off the set.

The two men gazed at the blank box. As far as they were concerned it was the same as if a bomb had fallen in their midst. They stood up and remonstrated loudly with Danny.

'What have you done?' one of them exploded, and then, turning to Donal with what I can only describe as a roguish cock in his eye, added, 'We'll never know now who won the war!'

Donal put on his famous grin and looking sideways he burst out laughing. As the man said, you'd have to be there. The two men departed. They had finished their drinks at the last bayonet charge and left us in a happy mood. Donal said, stretching his arms above his head, '*Do bhain mé taithneamh as sin*!' That cheered me up. He loved the ancient and neglected lingo of our land, and often engaged in Irish conversation when we met in the street. He was very proud of his part in Bob Quinn's film in Irish, *Poitín*, which was shown on television.

It was my loss that I appeared only a few times with him in the theatre. Tom Murphy's *Crucial Week* was one and *Waiting for Godot* was another, in which he and Peter O'Toole gave classic performances as Vladimir and Estragon. I was in the film *Philadelphia, Here I Come* with Donal and in a television version of *The Shadow of a Gunman* for the BBC. I played the part of Mr Gallogher, prodded and goaded into a pale reflection of authenticity by Donal.

I watched Donal many a time on stage and that was glory for me. I shall not forget him in *Faith Healer*, and there were moments when he sent a pang through my heart in Sebastian Barry's *The Steward of Christendom*.

May the sod rest lightly on him, and if he agrees to take part in a play in that actors' *alhambra* in the skies, I know there will be moments when he will break the angels' hearts, and when they have but dried away their tears, he will make them laugh again.

Solas síoraí dhuit a Dhónail!

Eamon Kelly is an actor.

Garrett Keogh

Goodnight Sweet Prince

'The bitther word again, Mary?'

There was a painting, 'The Vacant Throne', which hung for
years at the top of the stairs in the bar in the Abbey, a tribute
to the late F. J. McCormick. Dark and heavily framed, it
showed the famous actor standing behind a chair, script in one
hand, lighted cigarette in the other. A golden crown rested on
the seat, and the whole was surrounded by floating heads
depicting some of the characters he had portrayed. Coming
down the stairs one day, McCann glances over his shoulder at
the picture, turns to me and says gleefully out of the side of his
mouth: 'Here! You can tell them, the eh … the throne is
vacant no longer!'

During Garry Hynes' time the Abbey honoured Tomás
MacAnna by commissioning a bust of him in bronze. The head
and shoulders rested on a table in a corner of the bar and was
unveiled one teatime over drinks and speeches. McCann leans
against the counter and whispers: 'That's the best bit of
casting in the Abbey in a long time!'

Garry was directing Tom Murphy's *Famine*, and the word
was that she had brought in a dietician so that the cast would
lose weight and have a real experience of hunger. Donal

suggested the poster should read: '*Famine* by Tom Murphy, Starving In Alphabetical Order …'

'It reminds one of Homer's glorious stories of ancient gods and heroes.'

We didn't know each other very well, but we shared some of the same ghosts. The power and the glory, the pain and despair, the actor's life. The Abbey Theatre, and the echoes of all the lines and lives that linger there. The conversations carried on in quotes from plays.

We liked the horses. Going racing. Putting money on them.

And then there was *Juno*. I wasn't in it at the Gate, but I ended up travelling with it to Israel, Edinburgh and New York.

The Flowing Tide, six months before rehearsals — Donal had already been preparing. 'The only thing I want to do,' he says, 'is to get Philip O'Flynn's voice out of my head … He was so good. You worked with him, you know what I mean.'

'This is a nice nine o'clock!'

Edinburgh, and he's taking my photograph in front of a large stained-glass window on the hotel stairs. 'You're the only one of this shower who'd know one end of a horse from another,' he says. He scurries up and down, bends, leans over the banisters, and positions me so that I'm framed in the coloured light.

'If we go to New York … And I say if … the producers would like to take me out to the racetrack. Seeing as who I am, you see. Hold it there! Snap! What do you think, Belmont Park? Would you go? If I asked you…?'

New York, Sunday morning eight months later, he knocks on the bedroom door. 'Are you getting up today at all? The lim-oh-zeen is waiting!' 'Could you not have called me?' I say clambering naked out of the bed. 'Can't trust phones!' he barks through the now open door. 'Not with something as important as this. And anyway I had to make sure you were up!' He turns on his heel. 'I'll see you in the lobby.' Every time he said 'lobby' he reinvented it, as he would a line or a word in a play, and depending on the mood and moment it could be an appreciation, a critique or a full-frontal attack on the Americanism.

'Where are you going now?' he says when I get down. 'To get some money from the safe deposit box.' 'Ah here, it's the one day I have off, and I don't want to spend it waiting for you in a, in a … in a lobby! How much do you want?'

He loans me a few hundred, we get into the car and saunter off at our air-conditioned ease. I had been to the Belmont Stakes the week before and had lost enough to know my way around. I buy the equivalent of Turform at the gates. While others tan in the heat-wave sun we sit at our table on the balcony, have lunch, bet on the touch-screen machine close by, and look down through the cool glass wall as the winners pass the post. After four races I pay him back what I owe him. After six he asks me for a loan.

The driver drops us outside Paddy Bedford's apartment in downtown Manhattan where we're meeting the cast for supper. 'No, no, no!' says McCann, 'we can't go straight in. We've got to, to, acclimatise first.' 'What?' 'Find a bar or something and sit down for a minute. It'd be … detrimental to go straight in!'

Thirty yards away we go into a small, dark, local bar. 'This is better,' he says as I have a glass of beer and he another mineral. Then the door opens and we peer into the light as the shape of our host P. Bedford comes in. 'Sssh!' says McCann. We watch as Bedford is greeted by the barman. He asks for ice to take away, and a large one to take there. He raises his glass and our eyes meet. No one speaks. Smoke rises through slits of light. A fan turns on the wall. The ice cracks as it melts in his drink. At last Bedford says, 'I won't say anything if you don't!' We laugh, and then we stagger our exits so that we nonchalantly arrive separately.

'Did you hear of e'er a pub been thrun over?'

At that time he had a no-drink-while-I-work policy. Then the last night on Broadway comes and the drought ends. Within hours he's grabbing me by the tie and accusing me of spilling some beans on him to the Press. I hadn't, I didn't even know what he was talking about, but I'd seen this before. The broken jaw he got at the party at the end of *The Blue Macushla* twenty years ago …

Or the last night of *Juno* in Jerusalem when he tried the local beer for the first time. 'That's awful', he said, 'It's so weak you could drink it all night, take the breathalyser test and not fail it!' So he drank it all night, and at the airport the next morning he wanted more. 'Have you any shekels?' he said. 'For what?' 'Go down to the bar and get a six-pack to take on the plane.' 'But they have drink on the plane,' I said, 'we're going aboard now.' 'You do know you can't spend shekels anywhere else in the world, you do know that?'

Landing in Dublin after Broadway he didn't fancy the reception laid on in the Mansion House to welcome us home. 'What do they know?' he says. 'Let's you and me go to a quiet little pub somewhere and toast our own success.' 'It's only half-eight in the morning,' I say.

He looks around the hallway of the Mansion House. 'The last time I came down those stairs,' he says, 'was in a cardboard box. The porters pushing me.' 'Why? What happened?' The vision of him being ejected from some black-tie affair must have flashed across my face. 'When I was a boy,' he reassures me vigorously, 'when I was a boy.' Ah yes, the father: Lord Mayor, playwright, and dog fancier.

'Yogis, I seen hundreds of them in the streets of San Francisco.'

At Leopardstown one Christmas he asks me was I on the winner, a horse called Grimes. 'No,' I say. 'We were. Me and Laffan. At eight-to-one. And then, when it went out to nines, I went in again!' he quietly coos. 'Do you know Frank Grimes?' 'Yes, he was in the Abbey with you guys, the first *Borstal Boy*, has been in London for years.' 'Yeah. Well I saw him in Laffan's bathroom this morning. Just walked in to wash … there he was. In a manner of speaking. And that's why we backed him.'

He was amused by the rumours that were running round the town. 'You mean they had me in St Luke's before I even got there?' 'No,' I says, 'it was more like what time will the Mass be at in the morning!' 'Well you can go back and tell them that I'm not gone yet'. And in a rude display of health he leaps over the sofa to answer the phone.

'The statistics for advanced pancreatic cancer are very bad,' he says, sitting back down. He looks away like he's chewing something over. Then he looks back. 'But I don't believe in statistics. Me and God, we don't believe in them.'

He was concerned about his mare who had just foaled down in Wexford. 'Very important, the name, you know. Far too many of these horses going round with names … arbitrarily chosen. Just made up. Nothing to do with who they are or where they're from. No connection, with anything.'

The sire was King Luthier; the dam, Candid Lady.

'But I looked further at the pedigree,' he says conspiratorially, 'and the second dam, I found out, was Liquor Candy. So, between King Luthier and Liquor Candy, what do you think?'

Of course he already knew the answer, but he was going to take great pleasure in the pause of watching me wait. There was that sly charming look out of the side of his eye. The subverting threat of a smile. 'Well, what would you say to … to Sweet Prince? Ah? Good, ah?'

'When the swallows nest again.'

We're stood in front of the house — a big 1700s' thing with a daffodil-lined avenue, a lawn with geese, and a view over the flat lands of Louth. It belonged to friends of Paul Durcan. 'I reckon that Durcan is being good to me because he thinks that he might get an epic poem out of it!' He laughs, leans against the pillar and puts his hands in his pockets. Then he lifts his head, and just for an instant fixes me with an eye that almost says, What'll you get out of it, Keogh?

He turns back to the house. I go to leave. His voice stops me: 'Eh, by the way..I think, eh … Earth Summit. For the National. Yeah … Yeah, well anyway … Good luck.'

I backed Earth Summit and he won. I have the Lester Piggott biography with Donal's cartoon he did of me inside the cover. A few other drawings. A couple of good stories. There's another great O'Casey voice in my head besides Philip O'Flynn's. And I get to write the note I never sent him after *The Steward of Christendom*:

'Made all, drew clear final furlong, impressive.'

Garrett Keogh is an actor.

Pat Laffan

Dear Old Mate

How are you? Good I hope. Don't worry, I won't be indiscreet or tell any tales out of school and I won't say anything I would have been afraid of saying to your face while you were here.

After you had told me that things were looking bad on that Saturday in July 1999, I said, 'Don't under any circumstances leave before I get back from New York!' 'You needn't worry,' you said. 'I'll be here!'

Unfortunately I was late back — by one day. After the performance of *Freedom of the City* in New York, I put a few words together to say to the audience about you. There was a gasp when they heard and you were given a really stirring round of applause.

It was my deepest regret not to have been with you when you died. We had soldiered through many campaigns together for nearly 30 years. You handled things so well up to the last. 'How are you feeling, Donal?' 'Great, thank God!' I think you did not want people to be distressed on your behalf. Was it that good rebel Wexford blood? No matter that it must have been a miserable two years you put in with that illness. Courage.

It was always there in your performance, stretching the envelope — you gave audiences their money's worth. With ferocious charm and superlative timing. You never forgave me for cutting in on you that time in *Translations*. The pause went on for rather a long while and I thought you had dried. Unforgivable!

Back to the days of *Tarry Flynn*, etc.: 'Wait for it Pat, don't rush. Always go for the big laugh at the end of the line, not the little ones in between!' You stalked the text as a fox would stalk chickens in a farmyard. And laughs. You were not unknown for directing other actors onstage out of the corner of your mouth. Onstage you were the boss and were usually right.

Do you remember Co Clare, summer 1997, I beat you playing pitch and putt? My heavens. The next time (I think you must have made a pact with some otherworldly force) you played very well and succeeded in unnerving yours truly and beating me. Your grin of triumph was something to see. Like when you triumphed with the Christmas dinner! You were kind enough to invite me to join you several times. That was fine. But cooking in that apartment in New York in 1996 was something else. You were partial to offal and I'm not. You liked tons of garlic. I don't. You are in favour of undercooked meat. No way. Anyhow you were the boss and your play had just folded. What the hell! It was cruel to see your diet so restricted when you were ill. But you didn't complain. You used the time to discover new dishes. But bland.

I dropped into the little churchyard in Monaseed a few weeks ago. I still am unable to come to terms with the fact we put you there a year ago. Not that the mortal remains mean a lot. I can feel you at my shoulder right now saying, 'Get on with it!'

You know I often think we were fortunate to get through early adulthood at all. A bunch of young lads whose parents would have liked them to be priests, or civil servants or teachers, all hoofing about the stage with little or no training. But they were good times at the Abbey — Groome's Hotel where we had many an adventure; Molloy's pub in Talbot Place and the many 'locals' where you tended to have your banking done for you. We had the Opera Tavern in London and the wonderful Atlantic Hotel and the Kismet Club and the Queen's Elm in the Fulham Road. The Swinging Sixties and the Seventies and a good part of the Eighties. They were adventurous times and I followed where you led with great eagerness. 'So and so is a Catholic but a bad Christian' you would say. Frequently it was hard to disagree. Those who know about these things tell me you had a fairly profound knowledge of the gospels. Miles Davis the trumpeter used to say, 'Don't play what you know. Play what you don't know.' It sums up your approach to acting. It would have always seemed to the audience that they were hearing the text spoken for the first time — O'Casey, Shakespeare, Friel or S. Barry. Remember you told me that as you walked towards the audience at the end of *Faith Healer* you felt you could keep going. A rare enough thing to happen for an actor. Waves of love from the audience filling the inexplicable hole inside one's self. Stardom should have given you everything you wanted, but it couldn't and didn't. For a while alcohol did until you found it a false pal. You had that Damascene experience on Clare Island and after that you found some calm in your life. And you retained a kind of modesty and simplicity to the end. You would agree I think that when God hands you a gift he also hands you a whip — for self-flagellation.

You used to fantasise occasionally about giving up acting. Even though you liked to write, I don't think journalism was for you, or fiction, or playwriting. Some kind of artist maybe.

nal (top, left) with members of
renure College Rugby team, 1950s.

at Laffan took this photo of Donal
tside McNello's pub, Inniskeen,
o Monaghan in 1968; the actors
re on tour with *Tarry Flynn*.

As a young actor, playing Leslie in *The Hostage* by Brendan Behan,
with Maire Ní Ghrainne as Teresa, Abbey Theatre, 1971.

Scene from *The Singer* by P. Pearse at the Queen's Theatre, 1966.
(l/r) Donal McCann, Michéal O Briáin, Pat Laffan.

Scene from *She Stoops to Conquer* by Oliver Goldsmith, Abbey Theatre, 1969
(l/r) Leslie Lalor, Michéal O Briáin, Máire O'Ncill, Vincent Dowling,
Angela Newman, Pat Laffan, Donal McCann.

CHRISTMAS 1992.

Ma,

these are pictures of and by me.

The purpose of this collection is to make you think of me whenever you open it. Then, as soon as you do, you will know that I am thinking of you, wherever I am. Simple.

I love you,
I owe you so much,
God loves us all.
Never forget how much.

donal xxx

Donal's inscription to his mother at the front of a photo album he gave to her. A number of the photos contained within appear on the following pages.

A young Donal walking along a beach.

As Jean in *Miss Julie*, with the RSC at The Place Theatre, London, 19

earing the hallmark *Translations*' hat in Pat
ffan's garden, May 1988.

P. Laffan

Donal McCann (standing) as Phineas Finn, with Derek Godfrey as Robert Kennedy
in the BBC's production of *The Pallisers*, 1973.

From Bob Quinn's *Budawanny*, 1987.

From Bob
Quinn's *The
Bishop's Story*,
1994.

Cast shot from John Huston's screen adaptation of *The Dead* (1987),
with director's inscription to Donal.

You thought out your practical jokes, your cartoons, drawings, photography, etc., with the same intensity as you thought out your acting. Nothing was really random: an interest in horse racing, Scrabble, table tennis, pitch and putt, even spectacular drinking, all served in the search for clarity. Above all, in the work. Like James Joyce or Sam Beckett, you put in the statutory periods of exile — albeit in the Irish Club. With you it was the discipline of the words first and then the speculation to reach the inside of the author's mind. I think you reached a state of acceptance where you allowed the drama and life to play you. You'd say that was the will of God.

When we were educated, everything was done by the priests to snuff out self-regard. I believe they said at your funeral you had no ego. Not true. In spite of them you developed a very healthy one and were none the worse for it. If you had a motto it should have been: 'If you cut yourself bandage the knife!'

You wrote to me several times while you filmed *The Dead* in California. Being off the drink was quite a strain. You finished one note:

Frost last night
Hit oranges, lemons
Pray for this poor actor
O Clemens
O Pia
O Dulcis …
O see ya!

Pat Laffan is an actor.

Drawing by Donal, given to Pat Laffan, of the two actors as Hugh and Jimmy Jac
in *Translations* at the Abbey, 1988.

Tom Lawlor

A Gift Horse

Christmas was approaching with all its mad expectations. Our approach to the Gravediggers pub was lit like a runway with the fairy lights twinkling from the house windows. Inside Donal decorated the mahogany. Then it was my turn. Then he spoke. His old butty Matty was finding it hard going coming up to the Christmas. Donal had noticed the change that betrayed his circumstances. He no longer called in for a small one and a kitty and their daily exchange of runners and the jumping conditions at Kempton or Catterick was postponed. When he took the packet of Churchmans from his pocket it was a ten. 'I've no problem dropping him a few quid. But you know the story, his pride won't let him and anyway, I'm not supposed to know.' 'Could we not fix it for him to win the Christmas draw?' I suggested. 'Jesus, are you mad? The Christmas draw is sacrosanct.' We finished our drinks and headed back down the runway.

Two days later Matty picks up a note in his hallway. Please call Maureen in the bookie's office. Matty lifts the phone. 'Hello, Maureen, Matty Flynn here, is there a problem?' 'Oh no, Mr Flynn, thanks for calling. I'm finishing the books for November and I see you have some monies uncollected. Mr McCann is here, I can ask him to drop it into you or will you collect it yourself?' 'I'll be over, after I shave.'

Donal was sitting in the Gravediggers checking the runners for the day when Matty breezed in. He ordered the usual and lit a cigarette from a box of twenty. 'D'ya know what I'm going to tell you Donal? I think I'm getting the bleedin' Alzheimers. I had two-hundred-and-eighty-six quid from a Yankee lying down in the shop since last month. If it wasn't for Maureen spotting it, I think yer man would be off to Benidorm for the Christmas.' 'Maureen's a good skin,' said Donal. 'Ya better get a ticket for the raffle seen your luck is in.' 'I won't bother Donal, I'll leave it to them that needs it.'

*

The Final Score

There is a control in photography that is seldom recognised. It starts with the photographer controlling the subject. You tell then what to wear, where to position themselves and what attitude to adopt. During the shoot, good photographers transfer this control to the subject as soon as possible. When the subject has control it makes for a better shoot with better results. Hence good models make poor photographers take great shots of them.

The late Donal McCann understood the use of this control only too well. I first met him while I was shooting Joe Dowling's *Juno and the Paycock* for the Gate Theatre. We were using a room in Dublin's Henrietta Street to shoot some publicity shots. Donal was standing against the wall with his arm around Geraldine Plunkett's shoulder. The emptiness of the space emphasised the poverty depicted in the O'Casey play. Suddenly through the open door an unexpected visitor appeared. A small child crawled into the room. Geraldine's instinct was to go to the child but Donal anchored her with his arm and I made the shot. The invisible child in the O'Casey play had come to life and my friendship with Donal began. He dabbled with photography and would visit my studio when he had some film to be processed. In the darkroom he was a pain in the arse. His ideas of composition always differed from mine but he had a good eye. A picture of his mother in a nursing home was his favourite. Time and time again I would make a print for him, slightly changing the shape and tonal range. In the end we agreed that I would not take up the acting and he would not take up the photography.

Later I was photographing Turgenev's *A Month in the Country* at the Gate. Donal was sitting in a gazebo holding an orange. I was concentrating on the action outside the gazebo when Donal suddenly squeezed the orange sending juice in all directions. Afterwards in the green room he asks, 'Did ya get that?' 'No,' I said. 'One-nil to McCann,' he said. As well as squeezing juice he was also planting seeds. The idea was simple, a ruse that would have me watching him all the time while he was on stage, irrespective of where the action was. The score was to be levelled in the Abbey Theatre during Brian Friel's *Wonderful Tennessee*. Standing on the pier with his back to me with an overcoat draped over his shoulders he turned and released a champagne cork from the bottle. The front-of-house picture captured the bubbly and cork in full flight.

During my last visit with him we drank tea and discussed the final cropping of his mother's picture. He sat in the window with the light behind him. He gave me a picture he had painted. 'I think that suits you,' he said. Baby birds in a nest, a bird of prey and a phallus. The mind boggles. When it was time to leave I asked him what the score was. 'I think we'll call it a draw,' he said. Little did I know that it was also the final score.

Tom Lawlor is a photographer.

Hugh Leonard

The Way Things Were

To put the end before the beginning, the last time I saw Donal McCann was last January, when he appeared at the Maureen Potter tribute in the Gaiety. Mo and Eamon Kelly had just done a turn, both of them seated in easy chairs which were then 'struck' from the stage. Donal was announced and came on, looking distressingly thin. The first thing he said was, 'They might have left a chair.'

That, in essence, was his style. He was ill with cancer of the pancreas, and he would make neither a joke of it nor a tragedy. It was simply the way things were …

Thirty years ago, the Abbey, on a visit to London, where I was living at the time, mounted two productions at the Aldwych Theatre. The first was *The Plough and the Stars*, done on the fatal but ever-persistent theory that O'Casey was Abbey-proof; the second was Boucicault's *The Shaughraun*, beautifully directed by Hugh Hunt. It was not Cyril Cusack in the title role who transfixed me, but the dark young actor who played the romantic lead, Captain Molineux. That was my first glimpse of Donal McCann.

I returned to see him again later in the week, at the Saturday matinee. It would have been easy for him to burlesque the role of the young Englishman. At his first meeting with the heroine, Clare Ffolliott, he sighed, 'She's as fwesh and fwagrant as one of her own pats of butter.' It should have been mawkish; instead, it was as if he had released part of himself to merge with the character, so that it was impossible to know where Boucicault left off and McCann began. And later, suspecting his beloved of madness, he utters the funniest line in the play: 'It is the moon that affects her. I wish I had an umbwella'. He got his laugh, and although the actor soared, the English captain remained properly earthbound.

Unbeknownst to myself, I had a play already waiting for Donal: a two-hander called *The Au Pair Man*, which I had put away until I found the right actor. It was a satire on the British monarchy — rather heavy-handed in retrospect — and Donal, playing opposite the delightful Joan Greenwood, gave a star-is-born performance. It transferred to the West End and, late on the first Saturday evening, he and I walked to Leicester Square to read the Sunday notices. I opened *The Times*, *The Observer* and *The Telegraph*, while Donal waited expectantly, trying to read over my shoulder.

As I have said, the play had parts for only two actors, and I still remember my incredulity on realising that Donal was not even as much mentioned in any one of the three 'posh' papers. Even now, I don't know how I managed to turn and face him. The critics would one day give him his due, but they took their time, damn them. Maybe, as Joan Collins said, reviews are good only for wrapping fish and chips.

Meanwhile, he and I became friends — my wife and I gave him his twenty-fifth birthday lunch during the ten-week run of the play. It was the uncertain, hesitant friendship of two shy people. And, away from the theatre, we had little in common; he loved racehorses and greyhounds, whereas I did not.

Also, I think he suspected that I did not much admire the plays of his esteemed father, John McCann, which were wildly popular. Each one was a monument to the Theatre of the Happy Ending, replete with hard-chaw oul' fellas and loveable oul' ones. (I still recall an end-of-act-three line: 'Mary, Mary, it isn't cancer a-tall your sister had, but a little cyst, and it isn't malignant!')

Down the years, Donal acted in a few plays of mine, most notably in a revival of *A Life*, and — hilariously — in a farce called *The Last of the Last of the Mohicans*. In this he took the unlikely role of a closet gay: a pawn in someone else's game of amorous intrigue, who becomes more bruised and bloodied as the play steam-rollers over him.

I saw him in other plays and on television, notably in *The Pallisers* and my adaptation of *Strumpet City*. Once, in some connection, I referred to him in print as 'my friend, Donal McCann', whereupon, and to my amazement, he wrote to me as if this was a thing he had long hoped for but had not known for certain. 'Thanks,' he said.

Meanwhile, and slowly, his star rose. As a playwright, you knew that if Donal McCann was in your play, the dice were already loaded in its favour. He became unique in Irish theatre inasmuch as his name alone could fill seats. He could make a play of merit seem outstanding and a better-than-good play look like a masterpiece. No offence to Sebastian Barry, but I would hope not to see *The Steward of Christendom* without McCann in it.

His failures were as rare as hens' teeth, but there was perhaps one. I recall that in a dire 'Irish' *Hamlet* he was obliged to face down a barrage of sniggers on declaiming, 'There's something rotten in the state of Ireland.' And it was commonplace for him to vomit from a seizure of nerves before making his entrance on a first night. In time, there were stories of alcoholism.

His drinking was a form of rage, I think, and it gave the Lilliputians the chance to topple Gulliver. When he fell from grace a second time, a member of the then Abbey board — now departed to that corner of Purgatory reserved for begrudgers and slim-thinkers — declared with gloating pleasure, 'Well, that's the last of him!' It wasn't.

McCann came back, slowly and painfully. A few months ago, I said to him during one of our late-night telephone colloguings, that it was a shame that his stardom on the world stage had been so long delayed. I can hear his voice in my ear as if he were speaking now, in that inimitable voice with a faint tremor that might have been either a grumble or a heart breaking, when he said, 'Ah, what matter? If it had come earlier, I would have missed out on a few horses and a few jars.'

Tributes have, as the cliché goes, come flooding in. Many of them have been a search for new clothes in which to dress up old meanings. And there have been the superlatives that reduce art to a contest. Donal was the 'best', the 'greatest', the 'most illustrious'. He would have smiled. It was as if acting — like writing, painting, and composing — was an absolute thing, a kind of horse race in which he had galloped home in front of the field. Well, let me attempt a small appraisal.

Like any other actor, he came with equipment. He had dark good looks that could win hearts, a stage presence that in Orson Welles' phrase could 'displace air', that trembling voice that could shout or whisper, and a God-given timing. And there was something else: a quality that made him a one-off and that flew in the face of what to every other actor was an essential and to be cultivated. He had absolutely no artifice.

Acting, it may be argued, is artifice — technique, if you like. It is something to be worked at, honed, guarded, perfected. In the deeper sense, McCann had no technique. Rather, he walked on to a stage as utterly naked as if he were turned inside out. Every quality that went to make up the man was allowed to spill over and infuse the character he played. Tragedy, a sense of the absurd, anger, and, above all, sweetness and loveability were instantly on tap because they were inside McCann, and he never held back. He was honest because he could not be otherwise. He was an actor like none other, anywhere and possibly ever.

When he died, I took part in a small tribute on RTÉ, and it closes with Donal's recorded voice reading from Paddy Kavanagh's 'Threshing Morning'. It ends:

> *Maybe Mary might call around ...*
> *And then I came to the haggard gate*
> *And I knew as I entered that I had come*
> *Through fields that were part of no earthly estate.*

The truth and clarity of it made my heart crack. One believed in God, for there seemed to be no other way of accounting for McCann.

He was buried in a lovely country churchyard at Monaseed, that looks out upon the folds of the Blackstairs. As we saw him down, I could not wait to be home and watch him on my tape of *The Dead*. It was his best screen performance. And I remembered a *Newsweek* review in which it was said that McCann had to be 'the best actor in the world'. I thought,

Always the same tiresome horse race with its three runners: Good, Better and Best. Why not call him the *only* actor in the world?

Hugh Leonard is a playwright.

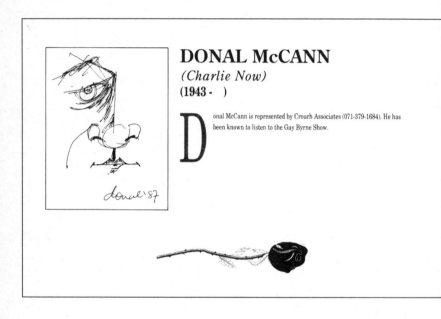

DONAL McCANN
(Charlie Now)
(1943 -   )

Donal McCann is represented by Crouch Associates (071-379-1684). He has been known to listen to the Gay Byrne Show.

Programme note from *Da* by Hugh Leonard, with self-portrait by Donal from the Gaiety production, 1993.

Fergus Linehan

A Talent Too Big for the Stage

From *The Irish Times, 24 July, 1999*

There is something about the Irish character that seems to breed actors in great numbers. Maybe it's the national gregariousness, the joy in language or just the native propensity for showing off. Whatever the reason there's never been a time, thank goodness, when a fresh wave of talent hasn't been breaking down the theatre doors in defiance of the rocks of constant unemployment, inadequate pay and rotten working conditions that await these hopefuls. Some of them sink without trace, some struggle on to make a living of one kind or another, and just a very few rise above the difficulties to become leaders of their profession and to set a standard for everyone who comes after.

Donal McCann was such a one, the pre-eminent figure of his generation, revered by his contemporaries as much as by younger theatre people. In this he stood in a line of great Irish actors that stretches back some three hundred years. His progenitors, as leaders of the profession in the twentieth century, include such towering figures of the early Abbey as Barry Fitzgerald, Sarah Allgood, and F.J. McCormick, while in our own time there have been Micheál MacLiammóir, Siobhán McKenna and Cyril Cusack, to name but some.

The sad thing about them is that, for the most part, as Keats wrote in his epitaph, their names are 'writ in water'. Pre-eminently, they were stage actors and their great performances ended when the curtain came down.

The cinema and television offer us some glimpses of them, but there are no Irish Oliviers to thrill us for all time with leading roles in great films. The international cinema, which so frequently prefers to cast a third-rate English or American performer to a first-rate native one, even when the subject is Irish, ensures that all too often our greatest actors have been reduced to supporting parts. McCann played in several movies, but in the main they were low-budget art pictures with a limited audience. He never got the chance to strut his stuff in a major Hollywood film and achieve the kind of international fame (not that it would have meant much to him) which his massive talent deserved.

Once or twice one gets some inkling of it: in his beautiful, restrained playing as Gabriel Conroy in John Huston's magical film of Joyce's *The Dead*, in Thaddeus O'Sullivan's *December Bride* and in Bob Quinn's *The Bishop's Story*, but though there were other good performances, they were in a minor key, and future generations will know him largely by repute alone. It was really only when he went to London and New York, playing in Sebastian Barry's marvellous stage play, *The Steward of Christendom*, that the world woke up to his greatness. Together with powerful monologues as Frank Hardy in Brian Friel's *Faith Healer*, it is generally regarded as his greatest role. Sadly, it was also to be his last.

In the end, it was the theatre that really counted for him. He had all the attributes for it: a face that was good-looking yet strong, with those big haunted eyes, a voice that was rich, yet with a strange melancholic break that made it instantly recognisable, even if you heard it on radio, and unique timing that allowed him to say his lines — even very well-known lines — in a way that managed to be his own, yet never to lose their force or meaning. He had also, of course, that indefinable thing called star quality. When he was on stage your eye kept going back to him, even when he was silent, though he never used it to upstage his fellow performers. The show was always more important to him than his own role in it. There always seemed to be something going on beneath the surface, intriguing stuff that hinted at tragedy even in his comic roles.

Truth to tell, he was in many ways a tortured soul. He had a deeply depressive side which, mixed with alcohol, could turn him from a kindly and witty companion into something of a monster, rude and abusive. He fought a long and bitter battle with his alcoholism and, in the general sorrow that surrounds his too-early death, it is a joy to know that he conquered it in the end. There was a time when one wondered if he was ever going to be able to work again, he had behaved badly so often, made so many enemies and got such a reputation for unreliability, the antithesis of his sober self.

But he picked himself up off the floor when Joe Dowling cast him as Captain Boyle in the celebrated Gate Theatre production of O'Casey's *Juno and the Paycock*, in which he gave a wonderful tragi-comic *pas de deux* with John Kavanagh as Joxer. There was a stormy rehearsal period with a minder appointed to keep him out of the pubs but, despite this, he was so difficult that halfway through, Dowling and the Gate's director, Michael Colgan, were on the brink of firing him. He was saved, according to Dowling, by Kavanagh, who said he would prefer to work with McCann, even as he was, than with any other actor.

The production was acclaimed as perhaps the best ever of the play and went to Broadway for a short run, where it received superlative reviews. The producers wanted it to remain on and spoke of it running for three years, but it wasn't possible and the chance went begging.

However, it's not true, as theatrical legend has it, that the reason it didn't stay was because McCann was unwilling to stay on the dry any longer than the three-week run. Other members of the cast had commitments and there were also difficulties in getting an extension because of American Equity rules about foreign performers.

Thereafter, McCann had a period in which he would go off drink during the rehearsals and run of whatever play he was in, followed by monumental batters, during which he would vanish for weeks on end. It must have been hellishly difficult to pull himself together again so often, but eventually he realised it was an impossible way to work. He finally weaned himself off drink altogether and was to remain off it for the rest of his life.

The poet Paul Durcan, one of his closest friends, says it meant a great deal to him. 'Never a day passed,' says Durcan, 'when he didn't say, "It's wonderful". Even when he was very sick in St James's Hospital he said to me: "Isn't it wonderful I'm not drinking. Imagine if I was drinking now", meaning he'd probably be trying to duck out for one in the middle of treatment. It was as if he was seeing the world through washed eyes. It may offend some ears today, but he thanked God for everything. He was quite religious in the old sense, a man of deep faith, as our fathers might say. But his faith had nothing to do with anger, that was reserved for those he saw as Pharisees.'

He didn't become a saint, though. Even after giving up drinking, he could be tetchy and difficult. When he was working on a play everything was subjugated to it. 'I'd get phone calls from him at one in the morning giving off about something or someone,' recalls Joe Dowling. 'And if anybody did something he didn't like during a play he'd mutter fiercely at them on stage. He used to terrify the younger players. I think it came out of a mix of personal insecurity and perfectionism.'

There's a quotation from *Newsweek*, much-used in the appreciations of him that have appeared, which always makes me smile. It remarked that McCann 'had an ego about one/twentieth the size of a Hollywood bit player'. The truth of the matter was that Donal's ego throughout his career was as thriving and flourishing as most actors', a necessary part of survival in a trade that calls on bravery most of us don't possess and where humiliation is always lurking around the next corner. What he never did, though, was trample on others to satisfy that ego and that is why he remained one of the most popular people in the Irish theatre right up to his death.

Tomás MacAnna, former artistic director of the Abbey, knew him from the time when, as a young man, he came into the theatre, still located at the old Queen's, playing his first small part in *Thomas Muskerry* by Pádraic Colum and appearing as Seamus Bond in one of the pantomimes in Irish which were mounted at Christmas. MacAnna speaks of his 'wonderful personality that filled the stage' and remembers him quietly going over his lines in the pub after rehearsals. 'He could be difficult,' he agrees, 'but all great actors have their difficult side. There's a nervous tension all the time that's hard to cope with. There was an eccentricity there, but the talent was so amazing that you'd put up with anything.'

When, in the 1960s, the Abbey moved into the premises which is its present home, he was one of a generation of young actors, directors and designers who, under MacAnna, gave the theatre a whole new impetus after the dreary years of exile in the Queen's. He played the title role in the first stage version of Patrick Kavanagh's *Tarry Flynn* and a lisping young British officer in Hugh Hunt's production of *The Shaughraun* — which was to revive the reputation of Boucicault as a playwright — and thereafter he was cast only in leading parts. Paul Durcan remembers how moved Kavanagh was by McCann's depiction of Tarry, who is of course the poet himself.

His end was sad, as all endings are, leaving his friends with the feeling that it was too soon. But he did find a serenity in his last year that was not always present in the rest of his life. Durcan recalls how after 'a ferocious operation, when he nearly died' his friend Kate Sweetman took him to her house in Duleek in Co Meath for five months. 'It was so moving to see him making his way back,' says Durcan. 'His acceptance was amazing. He wanted to know from the doctors exactly where he stood. He would travel up and down to St Luke's for treatment, always in good humour. He always had a great love of words and would do *The Irish Times* and *Guardian* crosswords every day.'

He loved horse racing and was forever scanning the papers for potential winners, looking for clues in lines or the titles of plays he had done. It was apt, therefore, that among the gifts which were brought up during his funeral Mass was a copy of

The Racing Post. He could draw well and used to present fellow members of the cast with little quirky cartoons during the runs of plays. I remember spotting him once, when the Cavaliers, the Irish theatre cricket team, got to the final of a competition, sitting alone out on the boundary at College Park. He had come to support the team. I went over to talk to him. 'Not bad for a bunch of mere actors,' he said in the sardonic way he had. (His comments, I suspect, would have been less than flattering about some of the more over-the-top tributes which were paid to him the week of his death.)

In the end, his main concern outside his well-guarded private life was with his fellow professionals and with his craft. Whoever composed his death notice for the papers chose well when they described him, simply, as 'actor'. It was what he would have wanted.

Fergus Linehan is a writer and critic.

John Lynch

Demanding Genius

I first met Donal McCann on the stage of the Queen's Theatre in 1963. We had both auditioned for the Abbey School of Acting and were meeting the other successful applicants for the first time. There were about ten chosen ones, quite a few who have had very successful acting careers, such as Des Cave, Clive Geraghty, Joe Pilkington, Maire O'Neill, and later Fionnula Flanagan and Stephen Rea. We sat in a circle under the demonic eye of the teacher, Frank Dermody, a small man in his sixties who talked at us almost in the manner of Adolf Hitler. Yet we found it all inspiring because he talked of magic, mystery and genius. 'When I was an actor I demanded genius of myself; nothing less will do,' he orated, 'Give me one genius and I'll travel the world with him,' he used to say.

Donal and I struck up an early friendship in a way that there was no going back from whenever we met over the years. He was working as a copy boy in *The Evening Press*. 'I work for the slaves in *The Press*, the sub-editors, you know.' Because he had a press card he got in free to see the Beatles when they appeared in the Adelphi Cinema that year and I remember that he was quite proud to have interviewed the Famous Four for a few minutes. 'I asked John Lennon if he believed in God,' Donal told me. 'He looked at me as if I didn't exist for what seemed like an awful long time, turned

away and mumbled in his best Liverpoolese, "I don't know".'
I think Donal was shocked by Mr Lennon's uncertainty but it
didn't stop him doing a brilliant impersonation of John Lennon
to my attempt at Ringo Starr in the Christmas pantomime that
year.

It was around this time, I remember, that Donal always had
a small bottle in his back pocket which looked to me like
water, 'Vodka,' Donal told me, 'To loosen up the women.' It
is easy now with hindsight to understand this as the beginning
of the slippery slope in which vodka was to play a major part
in the confusion and destruction that was to blight his personal
life and his career and which finally made it impossible for
Donal and me to have any kind of meaningful relationship. At
the end of his drinking days he was drinking vodka from a pint
glass and joking, 'This water is terrible stuff.' But in these
early days he was great fun, life was full of promise and we
were both dedicated to greatness in art. Donal fancied himself
as a painter as well as an actor and was constantly sketching.
Fame and fortune were never part of our aspirations then and
throughout his successful career the shallow trappings of the
business never interested him. Money was for putting on
horses and buying drink and that was that. He was always
falling in love and fancied all the girls in the pantomime
chorus. In fact he proposed marriage to a few of them and for
the next few years seemed to be constantly getting engaged.
He introduced me to his intended so often I lost count. We
went to a lot of parties together and I remember we were both
asked to leave a house in Drumcondra at three o'clock in the
morning because we couldn't stop laughing at an impromptu
rendering by the old and revered Abbey actress, May Craig, of
Mrs Tancred's lament from *Juno and the Paycock*. We

thought that to interrupt the merriment with 'Take away this murdering hate' etc., was a little incongruous at three in the morning, but everyone else stayed quiet while Donal and I couldn't restrain ourselves. We didn't know that this was May Craig's party piece accepted at Abbey gatherings for many years. Frank Dermody, our teacher, said we were a disgrace because we had no respect. I suppose he was right but it didn't stop him inviting the two of us around to his little basement flat in Gardiner Street a few nights later. 'Would you travel the world with Dermody if he said you were a genius?' I asked Donal. 'I don't know,' was his reply, 'He's a queer you know, it might be difficult arranging sleeping bunks.' Anyway we had a great evening talking to Frank. He inspired us with his quest for perfection, he was sensitive and perceptive — he was also a monster at times. But he was a major influence on both of us even though Donal discovered that he was spiking our drinks on that occasion. Donal had slipped quietly into the kitchen where Frank was getting more drink. 'Have a look, quick,' he whispered to me. Sure enough Frank was pouring some pre-made concoction into our glasses and putting water into his own. By using diversionary tactics we managed to make Frank drink the spiked stuff until he passed out. We put him to bed and went home imagining what evil fate we had managed to avoid. We both enjoyed the mystery and intrigue of the whole thing. Whenever we got together in later years Donal took great delight in doing a mime of Dermody spiking the drinks while carrying on a dissertation on truth and honesty in all art over his shoulder. The idea of the artiste's right to behave as he pleased as long as he was truthful in his art somehow attracted Donal and was to cause many difficulties for him later. It was all around us, many of the

Abbey actors were heavy drinkers, Dermody was delightfully mad and Brendan Behan was still alive.

One day Dermody announced something during one of his orations, which always continued uninterrupted even though he frequently fell off the stage into the piano in the orchestra pit. Coming up the steps, head high pretending not to be hurt, he said with great mystery, 'There is one genius on this stage today and that's all I'm going to say about it.' We all secretly thought that our guru had recognised our individual greatness but Donal was nonplussed by the announcement. 'Who do you think he meant is a genius?' I asked him. 'Himself, of course,' Donal said with a dismissive smirk.

Classes at the Abbey School of Acting were held from 5.30 to 7.30 p.m. under the direction of the aforementioned Frank Dermody, who had an association with that theatre going back to the 1930s, and had worked with all the great ones such as F.J. McCormick. I had only seen McCormick in the film *Odd Man Out* and thought he was rather good, but in the style of the little auld fellas in bowler hats that Barry Fitzgerald always played. I was more interested in classical actors like Laurence Olivier and in my arrogance, which came from a little talent and much more ignorance, I assumed that the Abbey actors weren't real actors at all. At that time I even thought Micheál MacLiammóir was a good actor. I now realise that MacLiammóir was out of date in his own generation, never mind mine, and that the intimate, simple, minimalist and truthful style of acting developed at the Abbey and conveyed to Donal and myself by Frank Dermody has had an enormous influence on both our very different careers.

I went to London within a year to study the classical approach at the RADA, acted for some time on the English stage, but have spent most of my working life as a producer/director in television and lately as a film director. In the early days Donal and I kept in touch by letter, chronicling my absorption into the English way to acting technique while Donal was becoming a star on the Abbey stage and developing his own way of doing things. I came back to get married to Hilary Orpen in July 1965 and Donal was our best man. He had grave reservations about my ability to carry the formalities through and was a bit miffed when I said I didn't want any speeches. 'Jaysus', he said, 'If you're going to make a balls of it, I won't.' So he bought a couple of books called *The Duties of the Groom* and *The Duties of the Best Man*, and read them out to me as he didn't believe I'd read them at all left to my own devices. Two days before the wedding, in the kitchen of his family house on Fortfield Road, across the road from Terenure College, he announced, 'My performance at the wedding depends on you, you can't turn up in your jeans and duffel coat so tomorrow I want to see your suit, the ring and some silver — a couple of half crowns will do — and we'll have to get a few quid for the priest, tips for the altar boys ...' He checked everything the following day, even our travel arrangements, and performed the duties of the best man to perfection with a wonderful common touch which endeared him to the older people whom he looked after and stayed with for many hours. When he was sure Hilary and I had left he made a speech which delighted everyone, including my father who became a friend of Donal's for life. 'You're a very conservative fellow,' I said, while thanking him some time later. He smiled and told me a little story which is quite revealing. 'You know' he said, 'I'm developing a reputation as a bit of a Brendan Behan around Dublin but I was put in my place the other day by a fella I was having a row with in a pub. He said to me, "Jaysus will you look at McCann, the only Irish Rebel who goes home every day for his dinner to his mother on the 54A bus."'

Donal stayed at the Abbey for another five or six years. He had many opportunities to make an international reputation, such as when he appeared, with Joan Greenwood, in Hugh Leonard's *The Au Pair Man* in the West End. and in *The Shaughraun* at the Aldwych, and later in *The Pallisers* on BBC Television. He told me it was a bit of a nuisance working with a beautiful West-End star like Joan Greenwood because he had to take a bath every day before rehearsals and become an expert on the new things called deodorants. He was quite embarrassed about perspiring but unfortunately the more alcohol he consumed the worse the problem became. He lived at the Irish Club in Eaton Square and had many friends, from Opera singers to building contractors, but his real passion, apart from acting, was for the dog racing at White City. Somewhere around this time I began to lose him. I had children now and wasn't as free as in earlier days and he'd become more self-absorbed. I also began directing radio drama at RTÉ, having returned to Dublin. Although Donal worked quite a lot in London in the early Seventies, he never really left Dublin. He loved the betting shops, the pubs, the people and they loved him too. He had a lot of time for doormen and waiters and was extremely generous to them. He had a great intuitive gift and connected easily with the most ordinary of people. At one stage he saw more of my father than I because they used to meet every Sunday in a pub in Terenure and go to the dogs in Harold's Cross during the week. In fact, Donal told me that they had agreed that I was a 'bit of a bollicks with ideas beyond my station'. He took great delight in telling me this because it amused him to think of me as anything but an actor. Yet we worked together on radio when I directed him in Sean O'Casey's *Shadow of a Gunman*, in which he played Seumas Shields to Niall Buggy's Davoren. It was re-broadcast recently as a tribute to Donal, which I heard accidentally while driving into Dublin, and his performance still stands up, he is only brilliant in it. We had a row during the production because I told him he was doing too much of a visual performance and that he would have to phrase it for the microphone. He got a bit annoyed, left the studio for a while, came back and said, 'Right tell me what to do'. I phrased one paragraph for him and he clicked right into gear and never looked back. He wasn't really comfortable on microphone or on film I feel, the stage was his natural home. But he did appear in a film of William Trevor's, *Access to the Children*, which I produced for Channel 4/RTÉ, Tony Barry directing. It was a difficult experience; Donal was unwell and although he tried to behave, the fact that he was playing an alcoholic didn't help. I well remember the day he spent a long time telling me the various tricks alcoholics use to hide drink and I didn't know if he was setting me up for a fall or he was trying to reassure me that he would last to the end of the film because he was betraying the cause by telling me its secrets. Yet his performance is a strong one and considered by some people to be his best on screen.

From the mid-1980s we met sporadically. He seemed more and more self-absorbed, yet would at times astound me with the depth of his understanding, a sort of physical presence that communicated a suffering beyond words and had a sympathy for all things living and dead. One of my great regrets is that I had not taken up a very generous offer made to me some years earlier. He heard I had written a play, *All You Need is Love*, which the Abbey was going to stage and said that he would play the leading role in it for me. Now he wasn't an actor looking for work, he was very much in demand, his name could fill a theatre. I wasn't to direct the play and I left the casting to the director. I didn't push Donal for the part; I suppose I chickened out and did not have confidence in my writing — it was a first play, and couldn't bear the thought of a cross-examination of the text from Donal. The fact is I could not bear the generosity of his offer; he didn't care if the play was a load of rubbish, he offered to do it for me. Nobody's perfect!

Although I did not see much of Donal during his later years I was so delighted that he had attained universal acclaim for his performance in Sebastian Barry's play *The Steward of Christendom*. I was also glad to hear that he had won his life-long battle with alcoholism and achieved a spiritual dimension to his life with much more certainty than the John Lennon of old. The day he was dying I rang the hospice and they asked me not to come in; they said he only had a few hours left. I went into the Abbey that night and was talking to Des Cave about Donal at the very moment he died, 11 p.m. on Saturday the 17th of July 1999. As we used to do, a few of us went up to Tom Murphy's house and that night we talked about Donal until it was bright. It was an unsentimental gathering for he could be a difficult customer at times we agreed. The story I remember best is a rather bizarre one of the night of *The Blue Macushla* party, or wake. It was a play by Tom Murphy which hadn't gone down very well and Donal was so upset by its failure that he drank a hell of a lot, and thinking a certain actor was chatting up his girlfriend, began to punch the two of them. 'He hit me as well,' added Tom Murphy. A senior Abbey actor hit Donal a belt which I'm told was not very strong, and Donal collapsed senseless on the floor. He was in such a bad physical condition that it didn't take much to knock him cold. An ambulance was called and he was in hospital for a week. The rather cruel story continues that Donal came to as he reached the hospital and shouted, as any actor would, 'Oh my face, is it all right?', to which the doctor replied, 'Your face is fine, Sir, but your liver is fucked.'

He was laid out beautifully in his old school Terenure College on the day before his funeral. Apart from a neat beard he looked almost the same as he did when I first saw him on the stage of the Queen's Theatre in 1963; dark-skinned, dark-haired, handsome, my friend Donal, who demanded genius of himself and whose wish was granted many times.

The only thing I can find from all the letters we exchanged is a programme which Donal sent me in 1966, on the occasion of the opening of the new Abbey building. The back page has replicas of the signatures of all the great ones of the Abbey past and present and at the bottom, in Donal's distinctively large handwriting, is written: 'To Bollocks Lynch with affection, Donal McCann.'

I think affection is the right word, Donal, and it was mutual.

John Lynch is a writer and director.

ack cover of a theatre programme from 1966, containing signature replicas of the Abbey greats, with an inscription from Donal to John Lynch.

Seamus Martin

Generous Heart and Hand

Donal McCann was a friend during the awful days of adolescence. We were copy boys together in *The Irish Press*. Our job was to run errands, make tea, collect galley proofs and act as servants for the important journalists whose names appeared in the paper.

We were unsure teenagers in a world where the egos of the nearest adults were immense. It was at that awful time in everyone's life when the surge of hormones left one utterly confused. Donal, I remember, was at one time unsure of his sexuality. 'I think I might be "queer"', he once told me. I, who suffered from the teenage boy's intense interest in, and immense fear of, girls assured him expertly he was 'all right'. The words 'gay' and 'straight' had not been invented at that time.

We went our different ways. I stuck with the journalism when he went to the theatre. I became at first a sports journalist and much later a foreign correspondent. Donal, the actor, never lost his love of sport. The horses were at the top of his scale of interest followed closely by the greyhounds. It was, as he once reminded me, in the blood. His father had, after all, died at the dog races at Harold's Cross.

His role as Phineas Finn, the Irish Member in the BBC series *The Pallisers*, was memorable not only for his performances but also for his stories of life as a young and rambunctious Irishman in London. A tale of dog-racing at the White City followed by a night 'at Her Majesty's Pleasure' was a favourite reminiscence.

At his great Gate performance in *Juno* in 1986, when it was impossible to get a booking even a month in advance, I was provided with a little chair to sit on in the middle of the aisle at the back of the hall. His portrayal of Captain Boyle was astounding. I remember not only being impressed by his talent but being overcome with a feeling of pride at the achievement of an old pal. We talked about it later. The success was, he said typically, due to everyone but himself. Michael Colgan was the real star. 'You know, he comes backstage and says, "So and so's out there. He thinks it's the greatest he's ever seen." Can you imagine Eoin Hand or Jack Charlton not going into the Irish dressing room at half-time? Can you picture them in the boardroom instead discussing what colour jerseys the players should wear? That's the way it is in other theatres, but not the Gate.'

In the old days in *Juno* it was all about, as he put it, 'Putting your foot down like an elephant on the laugh line'. McCann changed all that. It was, he said, about 'getting the right people, eliminating the negative and keeping the positive, getting an idea and following it through if it's right and leaving it if it's not right. When you do it like that with *Juno and the Paycock* it's a mystery to you that no one has done it before.'

In those days he was weaning himself off the drink. He was trying Kaliber: 'This stuff's not bad but isn't it a bit, you know, like inflatable women?'

95

Inflatable critics were not appreciated either. One journalist who rushed gushingly into print before a curtain even rose was put down mercilessly. 'I felt like suing him for premature ejaculation.'

We last met in Kavanagh's, the Gravediggers, in Glasnevin. He was as self-effacing as ever. When I brought up the theatre in conversation, he moved the talk towards horse racing. He was, as usual, embarrassed by references to his own talent. One felt he recognised its existence with trepidation.

Only once did Donal speak to me of accepting adulation readily. That, not surprisingly, was for an achievement outside acting. While filming in Dripsey Castle, Cork, strange things happened. McCann was convinced the place was haunted. The still pictures would not come out no matter where they were developed. This particular 'ill wind' was to the good of the actors and the crew. 'The spirits of Dripsey ensured we got an extra week's work,' he recalled. 'I celebrated by putting a grand on a horse. It won at 5/1. I remember arriving at the set. The crew all bowed pompously. The carpenters made a Papal throne to carry me round in.'

In the decade leading up to his death our contacts were by post. I had been sent to Russia and then South Africa as correspondent for *The Irish Times*. He, it seemed, was appearing on stage in every major city on earth except Moscow and Johannesburg. I did manage to see him, while on a visit home, as the tormented Frank Hardy in Brian Friel's *Faith Healer*. It is one of my great disappointments that I missed his portrayal of Thomas Dunne in Sebastian Barry's *The Steward of Christendom*. Not, mind you, that I would have got away with telling him how good he was.

Once I saw him, on a BBC World Service television, play with powerful restraint an RUC officer caught up suicidally in the Northern Ireland conflict. I managed to get a message from Moscow to Dublin to congratulate him on his performance. The following reply reached me by a circuitous route: 'Is that what you're doing over in Russia? Watching bloody repeats?'

A few weeks later I discovered a small parcel in the mailbox of my Moscow apartment. Inside was a copy of Friel's adaptation of Ivan Turgenev's *A Month in the Country*. Inscribed on the title page were the words: 'To Seamus Martin in exile, with admiration — Brian Friel.' I was stunned at first. I had never met Brian Friel in my life. My ego had just begun to swell when it dawned on me that Donal McCann's generous heart and hand had been at work to give warmth to the Russian winter.

Seamus Martin is International Editor of The Irish Times.

Maria McDermottroe

In Conversation with Faith O'Grady

I had known Donal vaguely since the Seventies, but I got to know him a bit better when the two of us went out to see John Huston about the film, *The Dead*. Donal and I travelled out to Los Angeles together and we were both very excited about it. I was up for the part of Molly Ivors and Donal was going over to discuss the part of Gabriel. It was my first time on a jumbo jet so I was pretty nervous and also a bit dumbstruck by the fact that I was travelling out with McCann.

I had been trying to give up cigarettes for about the hundredth time, but I ended up smoking on the plane and we both shared a few beers, though not too many as I know Donal was watching himself and being careful. When we arrived we were taken to the Farmer's Market for lunch and out for dinner with one of the producers. But, of course, the big deal was meeting John Huston the following day. We were driven up to see him and he started to talk to me first because my character was a lesser one. I knew he wanted to spend quite a long time talking to Donal. He chatted away to us, concentrating mainly on me and then we took a break and walked about the garden. McCann said to me, 'Well, you've got it'. He was a man of few words. I said, 'God, I don't know' and then, 'What about you?' He replied, 'I'm obviously going to have to stay on,' because that was being mooted. We were to do screen tests with them.

So I stayed on in LA for another two to three days for costume fittings and each afternoon and evening I'd meet up with Donal and either go to his room or mine. We'd chat and have a few beers prior to going out to dinner. We'd have a rota system. We'd sit and talk and smoke cigarettes and that is the only time I ever felt that I had seen another side of Donal. He could be very thorny. He was difficult to approach but he talked to me about his early life and the death of his brother. He used to sit at the end of my bed and chat. I think he must have been letting me in on something he didn't discuss very often. I felt uniquely privileged because he was such a very private individual.

When we came to do *The Dead* I left slightly earlier than everyone else as my part had finished. A small card was put under my door: it was a drawing by Donal, with the words, 'Slán Abhaile — Donal.'

Maria McDermottroe is an actor.

Marguerite McGillicuddy

In Conversation with Faith O'Grady

I came across Donal in 1981 when his mother was admitted to Ely Hospital in Wexford. At that time it was a nursing home as well as a hospital. Mrs McCann was there for 16 years and over that time, Donal would have visited her whenever he could. He'd always get someone like Pat Laffan, Paul Durcan or Christy Moore to drive him down as he didn't drive himself. He never really missed a Mother's Day. He'd bring unusual presents — beautiful flowers and chocolates. He loved coming down and would sit and chat for hours.

His mother was fully understanding of his ways. He loved his 'Ma' as he'd always call her. He'd send her cards or drawings that he did and would write, 'I love you so much Ma and I owe you so much.' She mightn't hear from him for a couple of months but she'd never worry. I'd say she did her worrying years ago. She was a very placid, lovely woman, a very interesting woman full of history. They were great to listen to in conversation. They'd talk about what was going on in the world and the past: Terenure College, Dublin and Wexford.

His mother was from Foxcover, North Wexford, and he loved that part of the world. He's buried there now in his mother's home place with her people. He used to visit there quite a lot. His parents are buried in Mount Jerome Cemetery in Dublin. There was about seventeen months between Donal and his mother's death. He was very sad when she died. He was on his way back from New York after the end of *The Steward of Christendom*.

He was a grand character. His ways were very simple even though he was a complex individual. He mightn't say anything for ages and then he'd be off and you couldn't get a word in. I understood him because of his mother. They were very alike and he was the image of her. His quiet, nice ways came from his mother — such a placid, unassuming, intelligent person. I learnt so much from her. She was a lovely lady. He had a great *grá* and admiration for his father too.

Donal was discontented and irritated with himself for years — a square peg in a round hole. I suppose the drink didn't help but I know he told me how happy and settled he was in latter years.

You know how in life you sometimes feel delighted to have met someone. That is the way I feel about Donal and his mother.

Marguerite McGillicuddy is a nurse in the Ely Hospital in Co Wexford.

101

Statue of Liberty with Barry McGovern's image below, in a collage
by Donal presented to his fellow actor during the US tour of
The Shadow of a Gunman by Sean O'Casey.

Barry McGovern

The Human Touch

From *The Sunday Times*, July 25, 1999

Humanity is the first word that comes to mind when I think of Donal McCann. He lived intensely and, whether in the theatre, on the film set or at the racetrack, explored every dimension of his humanity in his life and work. His sensibility was highly charged, and dangerous. Donal oozed danger. He could be the kindest of men — he'd give you the shirt off his back if you were stuck — and he could also be rude and menacing. It was this crazy mix that somehow, transmuted by his talent, shone forth as genius.

Donal McCann was a great actor, not merely because he was hugely talented but because his personality was so attractive on stage. He walked the edge, and that gave his best performances a daring that few ever matched.

Donal's greatest medium was the stage. You really had to see him live; he was never quite at home on film. I first saw him in an Abbey pantomime at the Queen's in early 1966: *Emer Agus an Laoch*, playing opposite a very young Sinéad Cusack. He was twenty-two years old and exuded charm and ease. After that I saw him play the Young Covey in *The Plough and the Stars*, Captain Molineux in *The Shaughraun*,

Tarry Flynn at the Abbey and Leonidik in *The Promise* at the Gate. In all these roles his magnetic stage personality won you over at once. The fact that he was also a damn good actor helped.

His fierce appetite for work and for getting it right was first brought home to me when I went to the Gate Theatre the morning after a performance I'd seen him give in Hugh Leonard's *The Au Pair Man*. I had left behind an umbrella or bag and remember hearing, through the door of the auditorium, Donal and Joan Greenwood rehearsing a scene over and over again. This was a key moment in realising what professional theatre was all about. It must be done right.

The following year, 1969, saw him play twice in Dublin with his buddy Peter O'Toole, in Shaw's *Man and Superman* at the Gaiety and, memorably, as Estragon in *Waiting for Godot* at the Abbey. Even then I was a big Beckett fan and this was my fourth *Godot*. Donal was only twenty-six but brought an endearing quality to Gogo which I still remember.

You praised Donal at your peril. He was always hard on himself and hated any sign of pretence. But recently I did so from a distance. I was touring with *Godot* early last year and I sent Donal a card from Toronto wishing him well and saying to him for the first time how much his performance in *Godot* in 1969 had opened my eyes to playing Beckett. I didn't expect or get a reply but I'm glad I told him. So often we never tell people we like their work. The greatest compliments I got from him were a squeeze and a grunt after a performance.

During the 1970s, Donal worked a bit more in television and films, and made carefully considered stage appearances. He played with Helen Mirren in a riveting production of Strindberg's *Miss Julie* with the RSC and with Anthony Sher in *Prayer for My Daughter* at the Royal Court and Project Arts Centre. In 1975, he appeared in Alan Ayckbourn's *Absurd Person Singular* at the Gate, Tom Kilroy's *Tea and Sex and Shakespeare* at the Abbey and in 1976 in Hugh Leonard's *Irishmen* with the Irish Theatre Company.

This period also saw the rise and rise of the darker side of his nature as alcoholism took its grip on him. His mood swings were often violent and he could be highly unpredictable. Yet it was this very quality — if that's the right word — which gave such an edge to his performances.

I played with him at the Abbey in 1980 in Tom Murphy's *The Blue Macushla* and Sean O'Casey's *The Shadow of a Gunman*. This was an interesting year for Donal. *The Blue Macushla* was fraught with problems. Jim Sheridan was directing his first show in the main Abbey auditorium with an unpredictable McCann playing the lead and Tom Murphy, the author, very present. A daunting proposition for anyone.

As it was, Jim was not the most organised of directors and Donal was drinking. In addition, there was severe friction between two of the other main actors in the play. The production never took off and closed after two-and-a-half weeks.

The day after it closed, Tom Murphy threw a huge party in his big house in Rathfarnham from midday on. Fatal. Much drink was consumed, people sang arias and hymns like Gigli and fighting broke out. A well-on McCann, who thought I was chatting up Fedelma, jumped on me and mayhem ensued. (I still have the torn 'Thieves' Carnival' T-shirt.) In the heel of the hunt, McCann was flattened by a robust Abbey stalwart. The party broke up some time later and Donal went to hospital where he was kept for some time.

Two weeks later, I met Des Cave going into rehearsals for *The Shadow of a Gunman*. Donal was to have played Shields. We wondered how he was and if he had been replaced. As we got into the lift Donal joined us, looking fit and healthy. As the lift was silently ascending to the rehearsal room, he laconically remarked in his deadpan voice: 'Apart from that, how was the party?'

The run of *Gunman* went well — and why shouldn't it, it being O'Casey's centenary? — and the following year toured to America, providing me with my first trip to that country.

After *Gunman*, Donal started rehearsals for Brian Friel's *Faith Healer*, which opened at the end of August 1980. This was probably his greatest performance. In the riveting monologues of faith healer Frank Hardy he seemed to come face to face with his own demons, seemed to 'whisper private and sacred things, to be in touch with some otherness' as another of Friel's characters puts it.

Throughout the 1980s and part of the 1990s, Donal fought hard against drink, finally conquering it a few years ago. During these troubled years, he worked on some television and feature films, culminating in his performance as Gabriel Conroy in *The Dead*, based on James Joyce's story. He also gave two of his most memorable stage performances as Captain Jack Boyle in *Juno and the Paycock*, and as Thomas Dunne in Sebastian Barry's *The Steward of Christendom*.

However, his talent, great as it was, was somehow unfulfilled. Undoubtedly his best years were before him. He seemed finally to have come to grips with his demons, if not fully conquering them. But had he beaten them completely, his magic might not have been the same. Somehow, seeing Donal on stage was a slightly voyeuristic experience. We shared his torments for a while, but we didn't have to take them home with us.

His many other talents included studying form (he was good at that), photography and painting. He was a brilliant cartoonist. I treasure a cartoon he made of me as Mr Gallogher in *The Shadow of a Gunman*. Donal, Des Cave and myself shared a dressing room during *Gunman* and the caption under his cartoon changes the line from the play, 'barring the children, it does be quiet enough' to 'Barrin' McGovern doesn't it be quiet enough?'

Donal was hugely talented, irascible, loving, infuriating, mordant, rude, loyal, generous and kind. He unsparingly helped younger actors. He was larger than life and yet a very humble man, always willing to learn and never quite satisfied. Theatre-goers of an earlier generation speak in reverent terms of F.J. McCormick. In our generation, and for a long time hence, Donal McCann will be the yardstick by which the rest of us are measured.

I'll miss you, Donal. I'll miss your intelligence and your wise silence. And your grunting, 'as if language no longer existed because words were no longer necessary'. At long last you have renounced chance.

Barry McGovern is an actor.

Abbey Theatre: **The National Theatre Society Limited**

Peacock Theatre

Lower Abbey Street
Dublin 1
Telephone 748741/2
Ticket Office 744505

Directors : Micheal O h-Aodha—Chairman
Tomas Mac Anna
Charles McCarthy
Thomas Murphy

Patrick Laffan
Gemma Hussey
Leslie Scott

Manager :   John Slemon   Artistic Director: Tomas Mac Anna

our ref.   *your ref.*   *date*

"Barrin' McGovern, doesn't it be quiet enough?"

Sketch by Donal of Barry McGovern in *The Shadow of a Gunman*,
given to the actor during the play's Abbey run.

Christy Moore

Close Cards

During the last two years of his life I was indeed privileged to have spent some great time with Donal.

It was invariably a quiet private time but we had fun too. He played his cards very close to his chest so I'll leave it at that,

Sincerely Christy Moore

David Nowlan

Artist At Work

The mere possession of a qualification in medicine can confer a remarkable sense of privilege on its holder. I will not forget the privilege of meeting the late Michael O'Donovan (more widely known as Frank O'Connor) when he was a patient in Dr Steevens' Hospital where I worked in the early 1960s. I even felt a sense of privilege when, as a young medical student in the old Richmond Hospital, I was given the task of escorting an immaculately dressed Brendan Behan from the waiting area to see his consultant. Brendan's behaviour on the occasion was as immaculate as his unaccustomed suit, and as unusual.

Working in the community hospital in Southampton on Long Island in New York in the late 1960s brought extraordinary privileges for a doctor in an area of the United States with more writers and artists per acre than almost any other part of that vast country. Who could forget John Steinbeck, with a forget-me-not plucked from a small bunch of wild-flowers beside his bed and tucked behind his ear, dancing around his hospital bed on being told that he was fit to return home?

I had put aside full-time medical practice in order to join *The Irish Times* as its medical correspondent at the end of the 1960s and had later been accorded the privilege (nothing whatever to do with having a medical qualification) of succeeding Seamus Kelly as the paper's drama critic. And so it was that I found myself on an aeroplane heading from Dublin to New York in the company of the Abbey Theatre's actors and stage crew who had been invited to Baltimore, Maryland, to present *The Shadow of a Gunman* for the audiences at what turned out to be a once-off theatre festival in the famous Mechanics Theatre in that city. Donal McCann was to play Seumas Shields to considerable acclaim in the production.

But Donal confessed that he had had an altercation a week earlier in Dublin with a toilet bowl which had somehow inflicted a gash in his posterior, requiring several stitches to repair. The stitches, he told the company manager, were still *in situ* and were due to be removed. I'm still not entirely clear why the drama critic of *The Irish Times* came first to the company manager's mind — whether it was the predictable sobriquet of 'Doctor Death' he had acquired since taking office, or the fact that his alternate description had been 'medical correspondent' — but the request went out for me to be so good as to remove the stitches.

It was a request to which I had no difficulty in acceding, knowing that such a procedure was neither painful nor life-threatening. It did not even require any medical skill and could probably have been carried out by the company manager with a small tweezers and a pair of scissors. Anyway, we arranged to meet in Donal's room in the hotel where we were all staying and, once it had been confirmed that the gash had healed satisfactorily, I was glad to be of some small help to a great actor. I cannot pretend that the occasion was attended by the sense of medical privilege that I had experienced when meeting other luminaries in clinical situations. In fact it was no more than a briefly awkward encounter with a friend I had known in Dublin at an occasional bar counter and had admired enormously on the professional stage.

I don't believe it would ever have been possible to experience a sense of privilege when in Donal's company, and here maybe I come to the point of this anecdotal preamble. From my experience of the man he would have sensed it instantly and then set about debunking whatever conversation might have been in progress. When he reckoned he had established some kind of equality between the conversationalists, then some real chat might resume. He never seemed to like the notion of celebrity: he was as uneasy with praise as he was with criticism. His innate bullshit detector was the most sensitive I have ever known and was never switched off. It was as sharp in its detection of what he was saying (he would go silent, seemingly without reason, when it signalled he was about to say something pretentious) as it was when others were talking. In our small off-stage encounter in Baltimore, he would be an ideal patient for as long as I was behaving like a professional physician.

His conversations were always fascinating because they were always exploratory. There was a sense of two people, on equal terms, wanting to draw information from one another. It might be an exploration of mutual experiences in journalism: his days as a trainee sub-editor in *The Irish Press* were often called upon, and usually with enthusiastic mirth. Others' experiences, maybe to be stored away for some future stage or film characterisation, were listened to attentively. Mental notes were being taken.

There were exceptions, of course. These were the times when his inner demons started to tipple with him and he would launch into a necessarily irrational and fearsome bout of drinking. The care and the courtesy inherent in his sober conversations would evaporate, to be replaced with a sometimes alarming bellicosity. And next time, when he had seen the demons off, the chat would be as cautious and as courteous as ever. There was never any flattery, never any self-pity. What you saw and heard was what you got. He was his own man again and interested in all mankind.

There was no false modesty, just as there was no false talk. There was a genuine curiosity in a man who genuinely wanted to find out, even if the curiosity sometimes had a mischievously cutting edge to it. And maybe that might have been why comments on his own work (as he liked to call it) were set aside. He already knew a great deal about that work, admitting at one time that he was an instinctive actor, acknowledging occasionally that he had a talent. But the talent and the instinct became bound and strengthened with a formidable technique with which the talent could best and most effectively be expressed.

And so we come, circuitously, back to the issue which first prompted this memoir: the sense of privilege. It was, naturally, a privilege to have known Donal; there is a sense of privilege in just knowing any serious-minded and talented person. But the place in which the greatest — the most exciting — sense of privilege existed was in a theatre where he was creating his art. He might not have liked the use of the word art to describe his work. He frequently said that he never had a career (just a job) — a person would have to have ambition to create a career, he argued. But he certainly had talent enough to create great art, and maybe that talent, that gift, sometimes frightened him. It certainly impressed him sufficiently to ensure that he honed his technique so that the talent could express itself optimally, and few will deny that he worked very intensively at his job.

That is why the ultimate privilege was to be able to watch him on stage in live performance. His every inflection, his every pause and movement, his every gesture and facial expression, informed by his intelligence and his emotion and even by how his audience was responding, added layers of meaning to the characterisation given to him in mere words by the playwright. Whether it was melodrama (he loved *The Shaughraun*) or comedy (in which his timing of a joke or a look or a move could add minutes of deeply felt laughter to the play's running time), his playing was that of a true master of his art. His Captain Boyle was at the heart of the success of Joe Dowling's definitive production for the Gate Theatre of *Juno and the Paycock*, and that is not to diminish in any way the huge contributions made by his superb colleagues in the production.

His creation of Frank Hardy in what is probably Brian Friel's best play, *Faith Healer*, was definitive and may never be surpassed. In his two minutely observed and exhaustively delivered monologues, he managed to convey insights into the state of man that most people had never even thought of seeking out. And his portrayal of Thomas Dunne in Sebastian Barry's *The Steward of Christendom* simply subsumed the entire text and sub-text of the play into his frail body and disordered mind, and seemed to encapsulate all of humanity and most of creation itself. Here, perhaps, was the greatest privilege of all: simply to have been alive and seated in a theatre to witness and to experience such greatness in the actor's art.

It was (although we did not know it at the time) to be his last performance. We are, and we will remain, bereft. But at least we had the real privilege of seeing Donal McCann make great art on stage for us.

David Nowlan is a theatre critic with The Irish Times.

Donal O'Boyle

Waiting for Donal

The standard image of Donal McCann is as Cap'n Boyle, strutting his stuff, aided and abetted by the jaundiced Joxer. The familiarity of the Dublin tenement and the characters were comforting, and I always enjoyed these performances. Comparisons are part of theatre and interval discussions remembering other performances were always an integral part of the evening's entertainment. This discussion was generally continued after the final curtain in The Plough across the road from the Abbey, or Sinnott's if it was the Gaiety. Was McCann better than Kavanagh, or as good as the last time, or any good at all, or was it all really worthy of criticism or discussion? To the last question, of course it was, and continues to be. The nuances of skill prompted memories of other performances, both on and off the stage, of actors and others playing out their life.

I emigrated to Cork in the early Eighties and, on a return visit to Dublin, got last minute tickets for *Translations* in the Gaiety. The only tickets available were three rows from the pit. The stage setting was taken up by a very large backdrop, and consequently the actors were close to the front of the stage throughout. McCann was the teacher. He was magnificent. He was so convincing as a hedgerow master, driving his pupils to learn the classics and forego the heathen English. He was in full flight of language and enunciation which produced a considerable amount of spittle. Three rows from the pit was within the range of spit. A warming performance.

My favourite memory goes back to the early Seventies. Beckett had just won the Nobel Prize and *Godot* was all the rage. There were productions everywhere. I cannot remember whether it was in the Abbey or not, but Donal McCann teamed up with Peter O'Toole as Vladimir and Estragon. They gave a stunning performance on stage. They gave an even more stunning performance around Dublin for the week as they remained in costume, such as it was. They were to be seen around Grafton Street and Baggot Street, in the Shelbourne Hotel and other watering holes, in deep conversation. On the Saturday of the week I was at a rugby match, of no great importance, in Lansdowne Road. There were the two boyos, leaning over the railing beside the Wanderers' Pavilion, sorting out the ills of the world as only companionable topers can do. Odd glances to the match produced grunts of encouragement to the players, followed by indifference as befitted their characters. As the match ended they, like everyone else, repaired to the Wanderers Bar. They were greeted with looks of astonishment from the majority who did not know who they were. This both McCann and O'Toole ignored as they ordered a jar. The barman did not know whether to serve these two tramps or to call the guards. Apathy prevailed and they were served. Such dedication to the trade.

Donal O'Boyle is an accountant.

Second sketch by Donal of himself and Peter O'Toole in *Waiting for Godot*.

Frank X. O'Reilly

Keeping the Faith

I think I should start with the words of St Augustine:

'You have made us for yourself, O Lord, and our hearts will never rest until they rest in you.'

I am not trying to do my priestly bit, taking the opportunity to preach a sermon at you. Through all the years of our friendship, I never preached at Donal. I never dared, but that did not stop him preaching at me and, I must admit, I was often in need of it. When I first met him, I did not realise that Augustine's words were so important to him. That came with the years.

I first met Donal in London, back in the mid-Sixties, during the filming of *The Fighting Prince of Donegal*. Bumping into him was just great fun and a constant struggle to keep up with his subtle wit. I remember, one evening, he described an incident at rehearsals on the set that day. He and some others were on the castle battlements as Hugh O'Donnell ran from the scene. The director screamed at them that they should react or shout or, at least, show some life. Donal did. Of course he did! As Hugh escaped, he shouted after the fleeing figure: 'Yoo hoo!'

Every evening we challenged one another on our ability at cryptic crosswords and at capping one another's quotations. He talked, too, about his time as a cub reporter with *The Evening Press*. It was then that coincidence, not for the first time, played a part in what seemed a growing friendship. He was very proud of a main heading that he had once come up with on the paper. When he told me what it was, I could not believe what I was hearing.

As a young priest, like many others in those days, I did a lot of work in amateur dramatics. Not very long beforehand I had rehearsed, with the parish group, three of O'Casey's one-act plays. When I rang the Performing Rights' Society about paying the appropriate fees, they said O'Casey might not let us go ahead, though we thought he had banned only professional productions in the country. They contacted him and, sure enough, he refused to let us go ahead, but Gabriel Fallon, the theatre critic with *The Evening Press* at the time, offered to do what he could to help. He even came to see me in Kilkenny and, knowing O'Casey well, said he would talk to him. The talk went on for a few days, with progress, or lack of it, being reported in the paper each evening. Gabriel even travelled to Devon to see O'Casey, but with no success. When the final report of failure appeared in *The Evening Press*, it was Donal who came up with the heading: 'And the Old Man Says No'.

I wasn't very long back from London when Donal's mother rang and invited me to Terenure for lunch with the family. So, on a few Sundays, I did travel up from Kilkenny. Did she think this priest friend might be a good influence on her dear son? Well, through the years, I would hope it worked both ways. Certainly he was a huge help and support to me in my own struggles with faith.

Coincidence re-entered the scene in 1968. Donal had a huge success at the Abbey in *The Shaughraun*, but this very success led to a confusing time for him. One lunchtime — I was a curate in Kingscourt then — the phone rang and my old parish priest came back from it to say: 'Get out there quick. Someone wants you in Dublin in an hour.'

It was the young Sinéad Cusack on the phone. She was in a pub on Henry St with Donal. He was feeling a bit muddled and confused about many things and asked her to ring me. I answered the summons, jumped in the car and arrived on the scene more quickly than I should admit.

We talked for hours, the three of us. Having had such marvellous reviews for his part in *The Shaughraun* (Harold Hobson had travelled over from London and filled *The Sunday Times* with superlatives about this new, young actor) Donal felt the time had come, perhaps, to go freelance. In the play he had been an *English* officer — with, of course, the most perfect accent — and it was possible that parts might be available now on a larger stage than Dublin had to offer. Too often in those days Irish actors in London, or further afield, were just slotted into small character parts as Irishmen.

There were so many things we talked about, maybe not all of them on that same afternoon. It bothered him, for instance, that he wasn't a few inches taller. It might cut him off from the young, romantic leads that he felt were his. I remember saying that I believed his greatest acting would come when he was middle-aged. The remark did not go down too well but, when it did happen, I could not resist reminding him of that afternoon in Henry St years and years before. He growled at me, 'Frank, it never happened. You're fantasising, as usual!'

I got my own back in Harold's Cross one day. He was struggling a bit with *The Guardian* crossword and I said, 'I have it nearly finished.' 'Do you now?' he said. 'Well, it was I who introduced you to *The Guardian*.' 'You did not,' I retorted. 'Do you know what you're doing, Donal? You're fantasising. As usual!'

It was 1968 and I said that coincidence entered the scene again. Donal was beginning to think of leaving the Abbey to try his hand in London. I was about to leave the priesthood.

It was not an easy decision, because it was years before priests began to leave in numbers. Somehow I had lost all certainties in Christ and in the Church. For me, the winds of change that Pope John XXIII had let through the Church were having little meaningful effect in Ireland and I felt that the voice of his Vatican Council was being muffled. I knew that I could no longer carry on, that I had completely lost faith. So, I packed my bags and headed for London.

I was teaching in a school in Chelsea, when Donal arrived in London a few years later. He was very concerned for me and wanted to help in any way he could, but that did not stop us partying, of course, nearly every night after *The Au Pair Man*. Maybe for us it was no harm that it did not have a very long run, but the nights led to long talks about faith and the Church. We argued. No, I argued and he preached.

'Frank, you have not lost faith. You could not lose your faith. You just think you have.'

'Go away out of that, you poor player. Go strut and fret your hour upon the stage. I want to hear no more.'

'Come on, you. We'll go to Mass.'

I doubt that I did, but through the years he kept an encouraging eye on me. And, after five years, beyond all my expectations but not his, I found faith again and stumbled back, a bit more battered and life-worn, to the Church and priesthood.

I was back in Ireland a few years before Donal arrived home and, for me, life was full and happy again, but, for Donal, the years ahead were not to be easy. The heart was not finding much rest, though he never lost faith and trust that, one day, it would finally rest in Him. And, though we seldom met, he still kept an eye on me. Now and again I'd get a phone call: 'Well, how are things? How is your faith? Are you behaving yourself?'

It was so sad that, with all the worries and problems of years behind him and another huge success notched up, illness should strike so cruelly. Yet, he showed an acceptance and courage that was truly exceptional. And he would still show interest in how I was faring, how I could live with people's growing distrust of the Church and increasing public rejection even of faith itself. He would say that my years away, 30 years earlier, must surely be a source of strength now and I told him a phrase I had been using myself in these last years, 'I have been where people are'. 'That's good, Frank. That must be a help to others.'

Towards the end, we talked a lot. He would ask for prayers and I said Mass for him regularly. Once, when he was physically very low, I said Mass at his bedside in Annesbrook. There were just the two of us and I will never forget his depth of faith that day. He was still hoping to get better, of course, but there was a total and quiet resignation to what, he suspected, might lie ahead very soon.

We had once quoted at one another:

We are such stuff as dreams are made on
And our little life is rounded with a sleep.

Shakespeare, lovely as the lines were, did not have the whole truth, we agreed. St Augustine had it better:

'You have made us for yourself, O Lord, and our hearts will never rest until they rest in you.'

Frank X. O'Reilly is a parish priest.

Philip O'Sullivan

Gone to the Dogs

My Dear Donal,

I wonder if you remember a day in January 1978 I think it was. *The Burke Enigma* was the television series we were about to film. You oldest Burke, me youngest Burke, with Kevin McHugh, Peter Caffrey and Larry Murphy the brothers in-between. The first day's shooting was Glasnevin cemetery, the funeral of our mother, and central to the plot. But it snowed and it snowed covering not just Ireland but the 'mainland' as well, in a not so film-friendly way of what seemed like two feet of the white stuff. Our esteemed Boss and our mutual chum Brian MacLochlainn cancels the day's work and by God we are free! It's 10 a.m.-ish and the Gravedigger's is just feet away. What to do …?

'Have ye any money on ye, O'Sullivan?' Not so much a growl as a querulous purr. Out of the side of his mouth.

'About ten quid.' A fortune for me at the time and probably subbed from the Abbey the day before.

'Jaysus, a millionaire. *Et moi, beaucoup de l'argent.* Let's go.'

The Pub. A real one. The theme, drink. Not a sewing machine or stringless fiddle in sight. Duck boards to an outside loo. Bar, gloomy, serious and perfect. ('Two pints please.' 'Ah! howya getting on Donal.'). I can't believe it. Just the two of us. My hero since I was six and my mother pointing you out to me, sitting in the back of a taxi, no less, crossing Tara Street Bridge sporting what looked like a very expensive fawn overcoat on you and your arm stretched proprietarily over the back seat. A god, verily.

Seventh heaven. Two more pints. Some serious silences, but not to worry. It's early yet. Elevenish now.

'Feck this, let's go to The Plough.'

A taxi summoned, farewells made and promises to return. An amusing journey to the city centre, you in very good form, pointing out this and that on the way. Giving me a Northside education you said. Indeed. The Plough Bar. Opposite the Abbey, our home. Colleagues rehearsing and us on the mess. Bliss.

'I'll be back in a minute.'

And it took not much more than that for you to saunter back, a look of some agitation about you.

'Large vodka and tonic, please. Tell us, d'ye know anythun' about horses, young Sullivan?'

'Only what John Gielgud said. Dangerous at both ends and uncomfortable in the middle.'

'Oh, yes, verrrry good …'

Another trip is taken. This time you quit my company with a gleam and a most determined air. A man of serious purpose. And back again, just as swiftly. A slightly dazed look on your face.

'Eh, how much did you say you had on you, Philip?'

'A tenner, Donal. Why?'

'How's your rhyming slang. National Dept., Borrassic lint, get my drift.'

'You, what? You've lost that amount on two effing ponies!?'

A withering sideways look at one so naïve and prissy.

'Actually no. On two dogs. Because of the *aimsir ou le climat* there are no meetings on today. Except an indoor dog track in Chepstow or somewhere. And the money is earmarked for Fedelma! There's a race in ten minutes and I quite fancy one of the mutts in it, for various reasons.'

'Are you out of your mind, Donal? That's all we have.' Stand firm. No way. So out you go with my tenner and the rest is history. A distempered hound. What surprised me at the time was what seemed almost like a sense of relief about you. That you had blown everything and now couldn't continue your spree. Quite literally spent. You were cleansed in some way. You became talkative, very witty. We talked, or rather I listened and was captivated. Theatre, actors, our Alma Mater, rugby. It flowed and it was wonderful.

And the remains of the day ... God knows. A quid borrowed from the barman, a taxi to Terenure and the family home, energetic negotiations with my older brother Charlie for cash in exchange for a voice-over cheque — crossed — I'd been keeping it for a snowy day. Thence to Blessington and the lakes. Your mood now starting to deteriorate as the realities of home, evening and explanations to herself loomed. Two more pints, and the 65 bus. You told me to sit upstairs at the front, with you in unsplendid isolation at the rear. My memory as I got off the bus at Templeogue was of two very dark and raised eyebrows in either dismissive or conspiratorial farewell. I never knew which.

There were many more trips for us in the years to come. Mostly your beloved Clifden. More apparent losses for you at the bookies, but nothing except gains for me in your company. And it all started and ended in a cemetery.

Keep well, my friend.

Miss you heaps,

Philip

Philip O'Sullivan is an actor.

Thaddeus O'Sullivan

Who Is Playing Donal McCann?

Donal. He had a way of putting directors in their place. My first encounter was a visit to his house to talk about the script of *December Bride*. While he studied form and watched the afternoon races, I rattled on about the project. Donal acknowledged my presence once in a while, just to be polite. Nothing much seemed to go in, but there was one challenge we had to face before I left: the drink, and the weight problem. To play Hamilton Echlin, a Presbyterian hill farmer from the North, a little abstinence was required. 'Yeah, yeah, don't be worrying about any of that,' said Donal. (Most actors' put-downs are a little more elaborate.) He wouldn't discuss it, but nevertheless lost several stone in a few weeks, and never touched a drop while we were shooting.

The day after we wrapped, I encountered the other, more infamous Donal. He had borrowed a box at the Curragh Races to celebrate, and since there was a lot of time to make up for, he took his *Veuve Cliquot* in pint glasses. An unsuspecting government minister who was sharing the box watched these antics for a couple of races and then leant over to me. 'Does your friend have a drink problem?' So I said, by way of explanation, 'That's Donal McCann'. By the time the last race was over, I found myself alone in the box with him. Word was out, Donal was back on the drink, and no one wanted to witness the end of the night. Neither did I, I was thinking, as I drove him back towards Bray across the Wicklow Hills. Then, as if from nowhere, a broken-down pub appeared at a crossroads. 'Stop!' Donal shouted. 'I know the fella who owns this,' and he staggered out into the night.

I was terrified of Donal for years. Gossip had set him up as the Dublin hard man, with a reputation to challenge the great literary drunks of the Fifties. But the other side of Donal emerged when we were on location. His sympathies for the project and everyone working on it were tremendous. He fell in love. I got the feeling he often did. And he passed sketches to women he liked — some filthy, some sentimental. He was sensitive, emotional and, in some ways, transparent. If you cared to look, it didn't take long to see that the hard exterior was just that. He used his own feminine instincts to bring subtlety and delicacy to the part of Hamilton Echlin, and enjoyed playing against the image of a garrulous and rough character. Such courage enabled him to subvert an audience's expectations and deliver a character of open-ended complexity. (We had to be a little selective with the feminine quality of course. As Donal the hill farmer sashayed across the drumlin fields of Co Down it occurred to me that we might have a problem holding the long shots.)

To my knowledge, he did not research, or worry about replicating emotions mentioned in the text. It was as if the characters chose him to 'represent' them, always retaining enough mystery to keep the audience intelligently engaged. And always with an honesty and truth, a simplicity, which was very moving.

Donal in *Faith Healer* was an unforgettable experience. He was capable of an uninflected style that was beautiful to watch. It seemed to me that Donal lived a timeless sort of life, as if in waiting for something. You could say he honoured that great tradition of actors coming from the outside: travellers, gypsies and so on. He kept himself in an 'untutored' state, ready to be a conduit for the next character that attracted him. He protected himself from himself (as every actor should) by excluding theories or intellectual examination that could not immediately be put into practice.

In film you often hear actors say 'I trust the director', as if that is the final test of the relationship. I never got the feeling Donal cared one way or the other. He may have had respect for or liked the people he worked with, but he was too much of a cynic to simply 'trust'. He was a true artist, by which I mean he believed everyone was in the service of something greater. He understood very well the combined effect of camera, location, design and his own contribution, and had therefore no inclination to dominate. He trusted himself to stand out appropriately. Many actors are quick to challenge the effect of the various elements within the frame on their performances and find it hard to accurately gauge their contribution within the overall scheme. These actors need to trust a director. When working with Donal I was aware that he listened carefully when I was discursive, and switched off completely if suggestion strayed into instruction. His consummate skill as an actor was to 'propose' things in performance, but never to dictate. There was no closure.

Donal's acting was a window onto something elusive, unknowable, fine, universal. Never simply the mirror of human experience. He was not the sort of actor who would illustrate emotion, expose his personal experience in order that an audience could engage, identify and empathise. So many actors reflect themselves back, and not the grand idea of a text. Donal had the courage to create illusions of character. In fact, I think of him as an illusion himself … an actor playing Donal McCann. If you suggested such an idea to him, with a sly grin, he'd probably agree — McCann the racing man, the bullying drunk, supportive friend, sensitive lover — except that he distrusted all theories. In reality he was an actor of consummate courage and freedom, who I don't suppose lived for anything else. And in his quest for honesty, I could imagine him subscribing to Cagney's great dictum: 'Find your mark, look the other fellow in the eye, and tell the truth.'

Thaddeus O'Sullivan is a film director.

Self-portrait of the actor as Hamilton Echlin (with ear phones), which he presented to co-star Saskia Reeves during the filming of *December Bride*.

Deirdre Purcell

A Tribute

From *The Irish Independent Weekender, July, 1999*

The public genius, the private pain have all been documented now. Even the inaccuracies have been recycled until every last anecdote has been spun out. The well of tribute may be dry.

I write this from a skewed, patchy perspective. I had great fun in Donal's company for a while but that was as an acting colleague and (relatively) carefree friend during the Sixties. He taught me how to cope with the scorching curry in the Golden Orient in Leeson Street, played practical jokes on me and on everyone else during the Abbey pantomimes at Christmas, brought me to dinner in Montmartre, the sophistication of which was lost on both of us because we were both so gauche.

I lost touch for many years, then got to know him again as an interviewee in the Eighties. He still fished crumpled balls of money from every pocket, still his jackets never quite fitted, but he was warier now and more closed in. A lot had happened, in public and private, but we both knew what was within and outside the limits. We could talk about acting, horses, scripts, odds long or short, plays, bookies, playwrights, jockeys, films, racecourses and truth. Or not.

He had refined his innate control of the agenda.

Our encounters in the Nineties were sporadic. Brief sightings of his jouncing walk as, cap pulled hard down over his eyes, woollen scarf wound, French-style, twice around his neck and *The Racing Post* jutting from his oxter, he headed purposefully towards the bookies at Hart's Corner. A pot of tea with him and Paul Durcan in the Gravedigger's, a pint of red lemonade in The Botanic House, a few social visits to Fedelma's house to see them both before he moved on.

A post-show drink in the Gate Theatre bar where I was lost for words, and this not solely because of what I had seen him do in *The Steward of Christendom*.

I always found talking with Donal difficult. Sport is of little interest to me and it seemed to be the only conversation, outside his profession, which animated him. To compliment him was futile because his own inner thermometer took the temperature of the performance, of the current state of his life, so accurately. And any attempt at social niceties drew one of those considering, withering, sidelong looks.

For a man who revealed his soul so honestly through others' words and who communicated so directly with audiences, he had few intimates. Although he tried hard, so hard that it was clear he desperately wanted it, he had small gift for intimacy off stage. Except for a tiny, tight circle of long-term and exceptionally loyal friends, he kept others at bay. Perhaps not deliberately. He liked to joust and dazzle with words, phrases and quotations. But frequently there was the sense that he was probing for something deeper.

To interview him for print — as opposed to radio or television which he saw as a performance — was to set off on an obstacle course of half-sentences, aphorisms, flicking glances and long, long silences. He deflected and parried with

133

the wit, with the eyes and with the restless, rubbery gestures, but even as you were laughing, dumped you in the silence. The only survival method was to go with it. To trawl through the words, to allow the silence to balloon until even he couldn't bear it.

He did dole out little rewards, now and then a straight answer to a straight question, occasionally a few seconds of encouraging eye contact. Yet even with a tape recorder or notebook in my hand, even though it was clear he was trying in his own way to be helpful — to me, to the craft of journalism, to the show he was promoting — I felt always that I was undergoing some sort of field trial. I always left his presence exhilarated but worried that somehow I had not come through.

Maddeningly, the journalist in him always sensed this. 'Now don't worry, you'll write something nice, you always do.'

It has been posited that he lived fully and congruently only on stage and it doesn't take a PhD in psychology to guess that there is probably quite a deal of truth in that. Acting is the shy person's revenge. It went deeper than that with Donal. Acting was his only possible revenge. He served it as art, used it as balm, covered his head with it when he could not cope with the world outside.

In its service, he was merciless with the fabric of his own body, mind and soul — but also with the sensibilities of others. This ruthlessness is probably how genius in any sphere or art becomes and remains genius.

As a result, the emotional truth of what he did on stage was instantly recognisable but confounds analysis. You had to be there. To see it and feel it. With apologies to Sebastian Barry, having seen the performance in *The Steward of Christendom*, I knew that night that I never wanted to see the play again. The performance was perfect, and Donal stored it in my memory as perfectly as an egg is stored in a shell.

We'll see no more on stage and although the films are the legacy, the performance was the life.

*

Translating Donal

From *The Sunday Tribune*, 17 April 1988, before the opening of *Translations*

Eight men sit on eight stools, a decent gap between each man and his neighbour, all facing pints and small ones in varying degrees of ingurgitation and watching the early evening television news. *The Star* and *The Mirror* and *The Herald* on the bar counter are dog-eared and well-marked with the name of the pub, Madigan's of Rathmines. No man addresses any other man until the barman turns off the television when *Newstime* comes on after the Angelus.

'What's wrong with that?' demands one patron belligerently.

The barman turns the television on again and tranquillity is restored. Three men move off their stools and go home to their tea.

Donal McCann walks in through the door. He has been rehearsing Brian Friel's *Translations* in the Leinster Cricket Club up the street with Pat Laffan, Peter Gowen and Joe Dowling. He wears a triumphant rabbinical beard which he fears might have to come off before opening night. He stresses things are not bad. 'Work is good for you.' He still loves the theatre passionately; it used to be half torture, half love, 'now the love has become more torturous or I love torture more ...'

'State-wise and masochistically speaking, I do enjoy it much more now — I work on it more now.'

He is forty-four years old. When he was a child, he got a set of Bako, a little set of building bricks made of bakelite which you slid down a scaffolding of steel rods, building solid walls, inserting a readymade window and perching a roof on top to make a little house. 'I remember trying to do it one Christmas morning and I tried to do it without putting in the rods — sounds like a lecture from a prominent Irish actor — no names — but I used to work too much on pure instinct. I start now with the text. I am now determined to know it, the words. That should be the starting point, certainly a terrific familiarity, not only with your own text but with everyone else's — it seems now to be what you should have been doing all along. But when I started out years ago, there were fellas looking for gold medals for actually getting the lines out on the first night.'

Still, if you asked the theatregoer in the street, the man who knows his actors, category-wise, Donal would be placed in the one known as 'instinctive'. And maybe the theatregoer might have a point. 'I'm quite amazed to be told how brilliant I was to get a certain aspect of a performance that never occurred to me to be the right thing to do at the time.'

Nevertheless, the 'instinctiveness' is based on hard graft, reading, reading, reading. 'It doesn't look studied but I probably work harder than anyone I'm acquainted with, peerwise speaking.' For this play, for *Translations*, not going over the top, not back to the Greek. Just the play. Working out a few things, unscrambling a few Frielisms, words, strange names. Charlemagne. Rhubarb.

Rhubarb is the international currency of theatre crowd scenes — five people orchestrated to shout rhubarb-rhubarb at the tops of their voices will sound like a mob. But even Friel's 'rhubarb' should be heard, every word of it — 'He writes great "rhubarb".'

There is splendid rhubarb in this pub, snatches of which, overheard from the next table around which sit a group of women, provide an intriguing real-life accompaniment to McCann's words which are swollen with long pauses. They are self-conscious only because he is shy and complex and while he wants to be helpful and truthful and to give the very best of himself, the self-critical third eye finds some of the sentences too revealing and lops them off. He sprawls and shifts and fidgets and drinks litres of lemonade, slugging them, four or five swallows to the pint.

Donal is talking about *Faith Healer*, Friel's great play in which McCann gave one of his finest performances. The women are talking about something else entirely.

'I'd love to do *Faith Healer* again sometime, but it's a very special operation altogether ...'

I got mine done in the College of Surgeons ...

'Optimum-wise, it would be with Joe [Dowling] and Ailish would come out of retirement, Ailish McBride — she married a Green or something, some colour ...'

I had gum disease as well ...

'Ailish [the stage manager] knew how to ride with a production; if you paused, or held a look, she knew you hadn't dried ...'

I had to get all mine out.

This play, *Translations*, is like *Faith Healer* all over again. 'It's going pretty good, I think, not bad actually ...'

My son-in-law had pyorrhoea ...

After the films, *The Dead* with John Huston (it was the third time he had worked with the director, the first was in *Sinful Davy* and the second was in *Mackintosh Man* with Paul Newman) and *High Spirits* with Neil Jordan, this will be a year of theatre. Following *Translations*, he goes to Broadway for a limited, three-week run of the Gate Theatre success, *Juno and the Paycock,* and will then go into a new production of Beckett's *Waiting for Godot*, also at the Gate.

Although he does not attend the theatre a lot — 'I do in spots' — he is very serious about it, 'too serious to go to everything. I'm not an agent or a casting director.'

Juno will start previews on Broadway in June but McCann has no desire to 'crack Broadway or anything like that ...'

Why not?

'Because I haven't — because it's a big commercial theatre which doesn't interest me at all.' The fourteen weeks of the Gate's *Juno* run is the longest he did since he was 'chained' to the Abbey in his early career. '*Tarry Flynn* for two-and-a-quarter years ...!'

The Dead was a tight repertory experience in some ways similar to that of a company like the Abbey on tour. Isolated 'in the middle of onion-field country' forty-five miles outside Los Angeles in a huge warehouse, the cast worked and ate together and lived nearby in that type of immediate and necessary intimacy. They hired a car once, because Donal Donnelly wanted to go into Los Angeles for the weekend, but that was a mistake because there were six of them and they were squashed.

But the intimacy was pleasant and since it was a short, eight-week shoot, very rewarding, since no one had time to get on anyone's nerves. And they were all very aware that this was John Huston's last film. 'The most important thing was completing it — not that he was dying, but that he was still alive.'

He loved the experience and he loved *Juno* and *Faith Healer* and years ago, he loved *Conn The Shaughraun* at the Abbey. 'It's hard to make out favourites.' Theatre in Ireland seems to him to be in a healthy state at the moment: 'There seem to be an awful lot more actors than there used to be. Years ago there were millions of novelists — now there are not that many novelists.'

He shifts and slugs and looks off into space and drips his voice — (the secateurs are ready to snip). 'Being an actor is now the thing, being a novelist is passé, style-wise.'

He probably developed his love of theatre by osmosis because it was probably the Da who introduced him to theatre, even though Donal was eleven by the time John McCann's first play was put on at the Abbey. He certainly remembers being brought to *Waiting in the Wings* by Noel Coward at a time when Dublin was still on the West-End circuit. He also remembers being brought backstage to see actors close up and to see playwrights visiting them after performances of their plays. He knew that the authors visiting the actors were conscious that there were only twenty-five minutes to closing time.

He did not go into the theatre straight away but into journalism (sub-editing in *The Irish Press*) and he still writes, although less frequently than he used to. 'I've nothing to write about.'

What about his life?

'*I'll* decide when it's over …'

Well, what would make his life complete?

'Death, obviously!'

He is also a very good caricaturist, caricaturing mostly himself. He has contributed to the programme for the Ian McKellen Aids benefit at the Abbey, a drawing of himself in one of the great disasters of modern Irish theatre — 'a production of rags and patches' — the soonest forgotten Celtic *Hamlet*. He stares out of the drawing, a pained and surprised creature like a black woolly marmoset, clutching a massive skull.

Yes the theatre is the thing. 'Most good plays will encompass everything — love, hate, envy, pride, sloth — the basic human condition. It's not bread and circus. It's education. That mirror thing. (The old catch-cry that theatre is a mirror held to nature.) A good play well done makes people think.

There is a sense of danger in the theatre — an entire body of seven hundred or a thousand people breathing together …'

He shifts so low on the leatherette bench-seat that he is almost horizontal but he soldiers bravely on. 'I sound like the man on the television who says it's a riveting experience — it actually is.'

As playwrights, he admires Friel and O'Casey (and defends recent criticism of *The Shadow of a Gunman*. 'It is a good play, it is just the unusual length that throws people.' And the poet, Davoren, is not unplayable — 'I think Des Cave was a terrific Davoren ...').

As actors, his heroes, 'globally speaking-wise' are too numerous to mention. 'I still adore Paul Newman, he is the perfect cinema actor. And Tom Selleck is really very very good. There are so many ...'

He takes another mighty swig out of the second litre of red lemonade and lapses into another silence. A silence with Donal McCann in Madigan's pub in Rathmines is not really a silence. It resounds with thinking and ruminating and retractions and considering and side-angles. Each new thought results in a new cast to his expressive face or shift of his flexible body or a fingering of the dog-eared script of *Translations* which sticks out of the pocket of his jacket.

Translations, which opens at the Gaiety next Wednesday for a four-week run, is set in a hedge-school in a remote part of the Dingle Gaeltacht in 1833 at the time of the first ordnance survey of the area when the bemused and confused English mapmakers arrive to translate the Irish place-names into English. On the surface it is funny and poignant; underneath, like all of Friel's plays, it explores more fundamental themes such as the loss of indigenous Irish culture with the loss of the Irish language.

McCann's name is over the title on the billboards and in the publicity, the Irish equivalent of Names In Lights. His list of theatre and cinema credits is now illustrious and never,

ever, tagged with bad reviews. There have been failures (The Celtic *Hamlet*) but he is never blamed. Since he attacks every performance with all his considerable heart, he is incapable of giving a bad one.

In that way, he lives up to an axiom of one of his directors in the early days of his Abbey career: 'If you're going to fail, *fail gloriously!*'

The late Frank Dermody was a small, irascible, inarticulate genius who goaded his protegés mercilessly. As well as being a play director, he was a teacher in the Abbey School of Acting who forced his pupils there into relaxation by making them fall to the ground off the tops of pianos ('See? I can do it! It doesn't hurt at all!') or by making them hurl themselves against the walls of the rehearsal room.

'TAKE CHRIST OFF THE CROSS! TAKE CHRIST OFF THE CROSS!' he would scream at someone who had not stripped his or her own emotions sufficiently during a scene and every actor present knew what he meant.

No one questioned it when he shouted: 'RED RAW!' He boiled over with impatience when gauche or self-conscious people were terror-struck towards catatonia by his ravings. He jumped up and interpolated his rotund messy little body between the protagonists in a love scene to show how it should be done. He destroyed the confidence of people who could not get on his wavelength but inspired people — like McCann — who could, and whose own talent and conviction could pierce the dross of the ravings to harvest the gold underneath.

One of the nuggets was the teaching that an actor's physical stillness on stage had enormous value. He taught people how to fill their own space so that their hearts and intentions were absolutely present for the audience. McCann learned the lesson well.

There was fun in the early days too, during the period when he played the *prionsa* in the Irish pantomimes, in the Abbey's temporary home in the Queen's Theatre, opposite Sinéad Cusack as the *banphrionsa*. McCann and Des Cave would enliven dead nights by allocating a word which had to be inserted into their lines by each member of the cast. Some word like 'elephant' which was quite difficult to include in an Irish-language pastiche version of *Diarmuid agus Grainne*. If the audience was mystified, they did not let on ....

After a turbulent start ('1 know I can't look at a beautiful curve to my career, but that would be boring — *boring*') McCann is reasonably contented now, particularly now, when he is doing 'excellent material with excellent people'.

'I don't know any happy man. Anyone who is happy is mad. Because of the whole situation, the whole condition. Anyone who is happy has a cast-iron certainty that he would end up in paradise and that is presumption and if you have that presumption you're back to being mad.'

In a far, dark corner of Madigan's pub in Rathmines, there are two men, dressed in well-worn, neat work clothes, one with a cap, one with a pipe, comfortably installed over their drinks. The company of women has left and the men's conversation drifts across into another silence.

'Mendelssohn, that's my man — and Liszt ...'
'And you know that fella, how do you pronounce it?
Boro — Bor-o —'

143

'The great thing is to be striving. Everyone's only doing his or her best — yes, that's what it comes down to, bottom-line-wise.'

'—*Din*!'

There was a minor problem looming at rehearsals of *Translations*. There was a run-through of the play scheduled for two o'clock the following Saturday. Catastrophe. 'What about the Grand National?' Mr McCann's eyes could not be more wounded and incredulous had he been told that fizzy red lemonade is bad for you. He had been thinking out how the director, Mr Dowling, could be distracted. 'We'll have to get someone who isn't interested in the Grand National to engage him in a long conversation around that time …

He is not a comfortable companion (conversation-wise), but even through the stilted talk there is always an excitement about him, an impression that he has a direct line to a horizon far away.

And there is never any doubt about the love that surrounds him. While the critics rave and punters adore, friends are fiercely loyal.

In the meantime, you can take the actor out of the pub, but not the sub-editor out of the actor. As he leaves Madigan's to go outside where it is still daylight in Rathmines: 'Write something nice — a small piece well-placed.'

Deirdre Purcell is a writer.

for Phoenix) *Laffan* . "*Translations*" — donal 17.5.88

Second drawing given to Pat Laffan of Donal and himself in *Translations*.

Bob Quinn

Dark Soul

Donal McCann's greatness as an actor had relatively little to do with his consummate skills and mastery of the crafts of stage and film acting. Many actors were as skilful. But very few had his power to intimidate and thereby control us. The nearest actor I could think of to match his dangerous presence was Rod Steiger.

In my opinion Donal's secret was a darkness of soul which, like that of most marked people, was based on dissatisfaction both with himself and with the way the world was ordered.

What often struck me was a deep and seething anger at himself and at the world for not taking more care. That may be the reason why he was fastidious to the point of psycho-pathology in his work. It was why his presence on stage and on film was so intimidating. He had seen the abyss in certain formative experiences of early life. What he did was not acting. It was real. It was why we were all privately afraid of him. It was why directors handled him with great care, why actors circled him nervously, why audiences watched, fascinated. This was a man in whose dangerous presence, off and onstage, we spoke deferentially, fearful lest we say the wrong thing.

Yet he could also be the mildest and gentlest person imaginable. Yes, he was frequently seen as a bully. It could be justified on his grounds that everybody should be as fanatic about perfection as he. But when he met his artistic equals on stage, the ensemble playing was electric. Ask John Kavanagh and Joe Dowling about *Juno*.

To meet him in preparation for a role was to be sucked into a single-mindedness that was alarming. Every word in his scenes — including the other characters' lines — was absorbed into his interpretation, which was probably why writers loved him. Ask Friel, Murphy, Barry & Co.

The young McCann I knew was outrageously handsome. His brown eyes and Jack Nicholson smile were fly traps. Susan Hampshire might testify to that. So might Sinéad Cusack, Maggie Fegan and others of his leading ladies. He was suspiciously tentative about his experiences acting with Anjelica Huston but he said he loved working with Billie Whitelaw. Thirty years ago I brought a young French woman — whom I fancied — to see him in the Abbey panto, in which he played James Bond. One pint after the show I had lost her to Donal.

Unlike many male actors, he was liked and admired by intelligent and talented men. Francis Bacon was one of his drinking pals in London. So was Peter O'Toole. Paul Durcan, Pat Laffan, Brian Friel were loyal friends to whom he frequently and fondly referred. He saw them not as 'actors', 'painters', 'poets', 'writers', creatures of an irrelevant demi-monde. To him they were real people who shared that precarious vision from which ordinary mortals escape into the day job. But the ones he seemed closest to were betting men.

McCann had a labyrinthine sense of humour and a sure instinct for comedy. Ask Hugh Leonard.

One of the interesting things about him was that he never became a tabloid star, despite all the necessary attributes. He avoided such a fate like poison though he could easily have done so and made a fortune. He was notorious for his stubborn refusals to let journalists turn him into an icon. Perhaps he had an ambiguity about him which attracted the thinking and deterred the unthinking. 'Why aren't you a Hollywood idol?' I once asked him. He said he never wanted to be a star. But he was human: when he saw signs of his old comrade Stephen Rea becoming a star — twenty years ago — he set alight the newspaper in which Stephen was immersed, in a hotel in Carraroe.

There is no doubt he was a sentimentalist. I know he could never accept the fashionable modern judgement on his father's plays — those that kept the Abbey solvent in the Fifties — which says that they were simply light comedies and would fail today. I would guess that one of his greatest and sadly unfulfilled ambitions would have been to act in a revival of one of them.

McCann was a survivor all his short life. In 1978 I asked him why he pushed himself so hard. He replied, 'To see how much I can take'. The characteristic of saints and madmen.

On location on Clare Island in 1986, Donal and the late Frieda Gillen, then 75 years of age, would rise at 5 a.m. and drink tea together. I don't know what they talked about but Frieda developed a great fondness for him, always asked for him and told me that he was a very religious man.

If you get a reputation for being an early riser you can stay in bed all day. The reverse is also true as far as his drinking reputation was concerned. He acted with the late Broderick Crawford and Niall Toibin in *The Championship Game*. Niall and Donal used to take Broderick for long drives during the day to keep the American actor sober for that night's performance. They weren't always successful. See Toibin, who might also recall playing sober games of Scrabble at night with Donal during the filming of *Poitín*. When he arrived in Los Angeles to make *The Dead*, Huston's assistant director took Donal aside and said, 'If you do a [named actor] on John, I'll kill you.' It was a reference to Huston's *Under the Volcano*, in which a main actor was clearly drunk all the time. Donal was exemplary on *The Dead* and worked with his colleagues to produce the best example of ensemble playing by Irish actors ever recorded on film.

It was not always thus. On *The Bishop's Story* in 1993, the early-morning taxi that picked him up reported a puncture. A half-hour later there was another puncture. And then another. When he eventually arrived, having toured various hostelries via Blessington, he was in a fairly dishevelled state. As he was being paid, the taxi driver handed over a half-eaten package of mints with the remark, 'He forgot his puncture-repair kit.' Donal always had a siesta in the afternoon. This time he took it on the steps of the Dominican Church in Tallaght.

He was an erudite conversationalist, extremely well-read and a brilliant user and punner of words. The trouble for a media interviewer was that he thought before he spoke. Andy O'Mahony will testify to that. I heard a radio interview between them. The pauses before answering were of Pinter/Beckett duration. Cliff-edge stuff. Nowadays such pauses would be edited out. But you couldn't have a showbiz-type interview with McCann.

His phone calls to me usually coincided with the end or the beginning of a project. They lasted a long time. He reminded

149

me of the definitive Bach player, Glenn Gould, who had a wide circle of telephonic friends and used to ring them at all hours. One friend reported falling asleep during one call with Gould and waking up an hour later to hear the pianist still talking. You could not do that with McCann. His antennae could read your silence. Nevertheless, whatever hell Donal inhabited became a semi-private soirée to which his friends were invited. One Sunday morning he rang me in a clearly distressed state to report the palpable presence of evil, and he was sure that Satan would appear. All I could think of advising him to do was to go to Mass and thus exorcise the feeling, because it seemed to me that religion was the source of his demons in the first place. I never heard more about the subject. Still, one always felt that one was the only confidante.

The only confidante … perhaps that was one of his acting secrets. His performances seemed to touch you and you alone. You were oblivious to the other thousands witnessing the man's sheer energy and effort in the cause of his craft, art, call it what you will. It was certainly more than acting.

It was his own very personal *ars gratia artis*.

Bob Quinn is a film maker.

Sketch by Donal presented to Saskia Reeves during the filming ot
December Bride.

Saskia Reeves

A Tribute

Donal was lovely to me. We wrote to each other for about a year after *December Bride* and then we lost touch. He and Ciaran Hinds took me under their wing during the filming. It was my first feature. One of the themes of the film was this triangular relationship between a woman and two brothers and these two actors and I spent a lot of time together. We'd sit in a tiny caravan, waiting.

Donal would have his walkman permanently on, the earphones tucked under his hat, listening to the racing which he loved. He was funny and eccentric, but brilliant and working with him was easy. I didn't really know what I was doing, but he made it easy for me. It always felt natural. He'd draw and take pictures all the time. He made me a collage at the end of the shoot. There is a sketch of me in the caravan and many self-portraits of him in other characters.

I miss him.

Saskia Reeves is an actor.

Brendan Sherry

McCann Finishes Strongly – Winner All Right

There were probably a lot of Donal McCanns, but I knew just two of them. One was a teenager, who went to school in Terenure College, and the other was an actor, who gave up drink and produced some of the best stage performances ever seen.

To his classmates, he was a rocket, setting off from Terenure during the early Sixties on an exciting, if sometimes erratic, orbit towards the theatrical heights. It is a matter of great pride to us that, when the engines that powered this special person finally shut down on the 17th of July 1999, he was back at base again.

Donal's teenage years gave some indications of the talent that was to later emerge. Being the son of a playwright Lord Mayor of Dublin, his interest in things literary, and theatrical, was to be expected.

I remember one extract from an essay our teacher had him read to our class of thirteen-year-olds. 'I awoke and reached towards my back pocket for my wallet, only to find the familiar curve of my posterior. I then realised that I was lying naked on a slab in the morgue.' Not the normal phrasing found in a boy's essay in 1956. After initial sniggers, the class waited for the expected reprimand. The comment 'Excellent description' taught us something of English essays, and

English teachers! Add to that rugby playing until age sixteen, taking up smoking at seventeen, and backing horses from an unknown age, and you have a brief pen-picture of the teenage Donal McCann.

Staying with the rocket metaphor, I re-entered his orbit, on a professional basis, in 1988, when he added a second accountant to his bow. Accountant number one had always been there, Mr Fogarty of course, who looked after matters pertaining to the turf. In passing I should say that, in later years, when Donal was nominated for a Lord Mayor's award (presented in the Mansion House where he had lived while his father held the office), he invited both his accountants to the ceremony. He always liked a good each-way bet.

That Donal made a significant contribution to the theatre is a given. For myself, much of my admiration is based on how he handled himself in the 1990s, after he went on the wagon. Anyone who has seen the damage that can be caused by alcohol appreciates the strength of character needed to battle back, once drink has had the upper hand. He won this particular battle in the Eighties and, despite the pain of those last months, there was no relapse. He was still undefeated when he died.

I often said to him that I would not have his job for all the tea in China. An outline of his theatrical working routine, in those post-alcohol days, illustrates why.

Get to bed at 2 a.m.
Sleep until mid-morning
Eat, and take a short walk. Be at theatre by 6 p.m.
Depending on location and make-up requirements,
    may have time for mid-afternoon rest.

154

Show at 8 p.m. Perform for two hours, for a few hundred people, and leave each one feeling that the performance has been especially for them. Do this regardless of how long the show has been running.

Finish at 10 p.m.

End the performance firing on all cylinders.

Ensure that times have remained 'tight' and, if not, arrange with cast and production for necessary changes.

Cool down and calm down, and do all that without having a drink.

Start again tomorrow.

And do all that for a laughable wage.

All of that he was more than happy to do, with one proviso: the scripts had to appeal to him. Taking work to pay the bills was just not an option. He absolutely refused to consider the consequences that this had for the likes of John Fogarty and myself.

He derived great satisfaction (as did friends and colleagues who had been with him through the troubled years) from the fact that some of this best performances came after he had stopped drinking. When he came back to Dublin in late summer 1997, having had a wonderful stage run in New York earlier that year, his health was starting to deteriorate.

In November he was admitted, for extensive cancer surgery, at the Adelaide Hospital in Dublin. His doctor had expected a four- to five-hour operation. He had to operate for eleven hours. Surgeons also fall into my 'not for all the tea in China' category

I saw a lot of him in the following months, and never once did I hear him complain. No bitter references to being knocked off the pedestal just when he had reached the very top. Instead he worked hard at dealing with his problem — tackling it at both the physical and the spiritual level. He said that his cancer had at least some merit in that it gave him plenty of notice of what might lie ahead. Those difficult days brought out the best in him.

During those last twenty months, he insisted that he look after himself. He built up a veritable library of cookbooks, as he looked for different ways to replenish his fast-disappearing energy. He worked out regularly with weights to build up his strength. His daily routine was a mixture of reading scripts, taking long walks, eating health food and making numerous visits to the bookies. However, he never did give up the fags.

Donal continued to battle on all fronts during the spring and summer of 1999 but, by July, he was very much the worse for wear. On the Monday of his last week, he had slowed down completely. He was just about able to get from his bed to his armchair, beside the telephone, where he sat for most of that day. He spoke less and less to his callers. On the Tuesday he asked to be moved into the nearby hospice. The good people there tried hard to re-energise him and, for a few hours, he showed some improvement. However, by the Thursday evening, he was in a coma and not expected to regain consciousness.

A sequence of events then took place that in retrospect reads like a script. Relations and friends were visiting, some with him and others waiting outside. At about 11 p.m., the nurse asked that the corridors be cleared, as a fellow patient had died. As if on cue, everyone moved into Donal's room.

He had been breathing with great difficulty, and the nursing staff had said that he could be like that for some time. Then, as we waited, in our supporting roles, the intervals between each breath became longer and longer. No one spoke. It is hard to watch someone die. Within minutes this true Christian, this great actor, this very private man, had left us to join his God. The circle was complete.

His friends in the Carmelite Order in Terenure College, who had so influenced his early years, took him in as one of their own. Waked him, prayed over him and accompanied him to where he now rests, with his mother's people, in St Patrick's Cemetery at Monaseed, Gorey, Co Wexford.

Ar dheis Dé go raibh a anam.

Brendan Sherry is an accountant.

'The Tallymen', inspired by Juno, given to Brendan Sherry by Donal.

Tommy Smith

In Conversation with Faith O'Grady

Donal McCann's death was a shock, although I knew he was
seriously ill. Nevertheless I was unprepared when it happened.
I knew Donal for a long number of years. I first recall his great
speaking voice which at no time was more powerful than in
his portrayal of *Tarry Flynn*. Donal was an actor and acting
was his work and talking about his work was not what he
wanted to do when we met. He used to say, 'It's only a bore
that goes out to talk about their work'. When he called, he had
his coffee and a chat. Usually he set the tone and topic of
discussion.

He loved to look at the art on display in Grogan's. He
would converse with the artists about their pictures. He
regularly had work on display and was a very competent artist.
When his work sold he would donate the money to charity, all
without fuss. We would enjoy his quirky and interesting
artistic pieces. The Beckett influence and the Joycean tone
were a great talking point. Donal was also a good poet. Some
of his poems were published in *Martello*, a literary magazine.
His illustrations were sometimes in the same magazine. He is
featured in a stained-glass panel on permanent display in this
pub, done by Katherine Lamb. I recall his friendship with
Seamus Scully from Moore Street who was the quintessential
Dubliner. Scully was a great first-night theatre-goer and he

was one of Donal's greatest critics and admirers. They would discuss theatre and film and their discussions would be intense and heated. Scully would want to talk about Donal's father, the playwright, and other people like Sean O'Casey with whom he had a long correspondence. Donal had to respect your views and the person before he would engage in 'work-talk', as he called it.

He was very well read and would often talk about poetry. He even talked about writing a book himself.

I really enjoyed his performance in *The Dead* because I think his heart entered into it. He was very much a Joycean individual. He was like Bloom, slipping in to Grogan's, Neary's, the bookies, up and down the street. He was always on his own and never had an entourage in his life. He didn't invite you to come with him.

He loved his city more than anything else and also the sensitive side of the Dubliner. Dubliners tend to be sensitive, sentimental and community-based — although not as much as they used to be. They were always careful not to say too much against each other. You found out more about Donal from what he didn't say than from what he did say. Rather than expressing a criticism, he would shrug his shoulders. He was an understanding human being.

Tommy Smith owns Grogan's pub.

Front and back of postcard featuring a photo taken by Donal of John Kavanagh in his dressing room, during the 1990 production of *Juno and the Paycock* by Sean O'Casey. Underneath is Donal's inscription to his bookie.

BY THE TIME YOU GET THIS, I MAY NEED THE PRICE OF THE STAMP. HAVE A REASONABLE 1991.

donal McGrann

John Kavanagh (left) as Joxer Daly and Donal McCann as Captain Jack Boyle in *Juno and the Paycock* at the Gate, 1986.

Juno cast outside a Henrietta Street building. (l/r) Maureen Potter as Maisie Madigan,
Geraldine Plunkett as Juno, Donal McCann as Captain Jack Boyle,
John Kavanagh as Joxer Daly.

Above and opposite: Donal as Thomas Dunne in Sebastian Barry's
The Steward of Christendom, 1996.

As Terry in *Wonderful Tennessee* by Brian Friel, at the Gate, 1993.
With this image, Tom Lawlor captures a moment and evens a score (p. 69).

On the day of Donal's conferring at Trinity College in 1997, having received an honorary doctorate from the university (see p. 202).

B. Sherry

With Paul Durcan (left) and Brian Friel on graduation day.

Donal, looking relaxed in his home, two months before he die

Jog

by Donal McCann
(For B.K.)

Talons were gouging my face
I clawed them away
– she'd never harm you –
a strange voice said.

At the end of the bed
stood a giant priest
with on either shoulder
a budgerigar and a silver dove
in his lapel.

I tried to ask him
what he was doing
in Hell.

19 July 1990
Published in Martello, *winter 1992*

Max Stafford-Clark

Revealing Performance

By the time *The Steward of Christendom* opened in Dublin it had already enjoyed a brief run with excellent notices in the Royal Court's Theatre Upstairs. Both the play and Donal's performance had been acclaimed so I was less apprehensive at the Gate's opening night than perhaps I should have been. Dublin makes up its own mind on these occasions without any help from London. But the Gate was packed and Donal was in top form.

Nudity is always a particularly sensitive issue in Dublin and I remembered *A Prayer for My Daughter* in the Dublin Festival of 1979, where Donal had embraced and enfolded a stark-naked Kevin McNally. The tender image crackled with tension and Festival Director Hugh Leonard, who had looked in on the production in the course of his rounds, was unable to leave lest it be construed as a gesture of disapproval. In *The Steward of Christendom* the scene where Thomas Dunne is stripped naked and washed by the warder, Smith, went well. Donal ended the long first-half with the wrenching story of his wife's death in childbirth. It was always a crucial moment and demanded as much from the audience as it did from Donal. The first-half set up the Dunne family and the situation while the second-half delivered the most moving climax.

The interval arrived and I panicked in the face of the packed bar and the interval chat. I scurried down the steps and out into the faded elegance of Parnell Square where I sheltered behind a pillar. Behind me came two women in their thirties who were keen for a fag. As they lit up I tuned into their half-time verdict.

'Well,' said one thoughtfully in a cultivated Dublin accent, 'he's not a thin man.'

'Ah, go on Margaret,' said the other. 'I wouldn't say no and neither would you.'

I recounted this conversation at notes the next day. Donal claimed it was an aesthetic verdict based on performance rather than physique. And so it was.

Max Stafford-Clark is a theatre director.

Line drawing by Donal of himself as Thomas Dunne in *The Steward of Christendom* by Sebastian Barry, subsequently used by the Royal Court Theatre as a postcard.

Gerry Stembridge

An Interview

Interview, published in *Film West*, between Gerry Stembridge and Donal McCann, filmed at Galway Film Fleadh, 1999, as part of the documentary *It Must Be Done Right*.

Gerry Stembridge: If we all gathered together by accident and I said I wanted to talk to someone from Irish theatre and Irish film I don't think it would take us very long to choose the person we would most like to talk to, and luckily that person is here (laughs) — Ladies and Gentlemen, welcome Donal McCann.

Michael D. Higgins let the cat out of the bag last night so we better start at the very beginning: tell us about Cordelia? You played Cordelia?

Donal McCann: I did …

GS: Were you a pretty lad?

DMcC: So they tell me. That was pretty good except at the same time I was on the JCT [Junior Cup Team] playing rugby. Cordelia in the middle of the front row is dodgy if you have boarders in the second row (laughs) — it was very good. And there was an excellent King Lear, who went on to become a doctor unfortunately, called Philip Williams, and Regan in that

165

was Frank Dunne who was the very well-known bass baritone singer, and Mike Murphy was in it … as the bastard! (laughs) He had the nicest speaking voice and it was a huge hit and ran for three nights.

GS: For someone like myself, not from Dublin, I always think of places like Terenure College as rugby schools, but it had a big drama tradition as well?

DMcC: Yeah, well Maurice Good was a professional actor, many years before me. They had a very good past pupils' group and we were inclined to say that so-and-so would have been terrific if he'd taken it up. Bertie Church was one. He was a good few years older than I was and he was a fabulously gifted actor, the kind of guy who would not get the extra laugh for the sake of the play — if you follow me — he was quite happy with one where it was intended … mind you people like that are quite rare anyway.

GS: This is a personal question: Terenure College in the Fifties — would you have got much encouragement to be a professional actor or what was it like to feel that in your head, 'That's what I want to be, that's what I want to do'?

DMcC: Well, they had a great tradition to do with Shakespeare and they did a lot of good productions and they had a series of talented priests, brothers and that. Fr Hannigan was the man when I was there and they were really committed to doing the thing well and they weren't looking for a big break, to be invited to do Glenstal or anything like that (laughs). It wasn't a career thing and so they encouraged it … There wasn't an attitude of 'Oh, you're terrific in this but don't forget you're going to have to get a real job afterwards'.

166

I didn't know anything really about it. I was thinking I'd like to be in the theatre when I left school, I thought that would be a good thing — or be an actor — I hadn't a clue really, but one of the sternest priests at the time was Fr Grace, the science teacher — I'd been Cordelia and then Malvolio, then cruelly overlooked as Hamlet and I was made play Polonius which of course I enjoyed much more on the professional grounds of Fr Hannigan that 'anyone can play fucking Hamlet'. Which was a clever move — he would have been a good producer, God rest him, he was a great guy. Well, I bought it and played Polonius and stopped sulking …

GS: And you got most of the laughs I presume?

DMcC: I got the extra one … yeah, that's where I learned not to do that. It upset the guy playing Ophelia something terrible and I realised I should never, ever do that again and I don't think I have … though I'm sure there are people here who would say 'Oh yes you did'. But conscience-wise I don't think I have. But I was going to say about Fr Grace, at the end when they say, 'Are you going to take the Honours paper or the Pass paper, this kind of formality, and all the good guys (raises hand) say 'Well I think I'll try the Honours' and I said 'Well I think I'll try the Pass' and he said 'Sure what good will that be to an actor anyway?' and he wasn't being dismissive or anything. He was just saying 'Turn up and do it anyway'. And that really put something into my head, that people actually saw the thing as a job because I thought it was impossible. I had no idea how to become an employed actor or even to go about learning to be a professional actor.

GS: So it was the teachers?

DMcC: Yeah, and I realised that that echoed the opinions of other people as well …

GS: Which is a particularly Irish thing isn't it — not willing to step out and say those things?

DMcC: That's right, and I think in retrospect they were very very good and put absolutely nothing in your way and if you had trouble learning your lines with a play coming up, you could get out of a French class or something to really swot up on it … you know, sensible.

GS: So you had three Shakespeares or something under your belt by the time you left?

DMcC: Yeah, quite enough, it was terrific …

GS: I was glancing around earlier and think there's quite a few actors here coming from acting schools and the university acting schools. What was the route for you that made you want to pursue this?

DMcC: Well, the proven route for me was to go and study architecture in Bolton Street … (laughs)

GS: Tips from Donal McCann.

DMcC: And you make a complete bollox of that — you get thrown out by insisting on referring to a board as a plank. That eventually rankles so badly with the building construction teachers that they report you and there's a question of your whole seriousness and you leave, shortly before Robert Ballagh. He learned a lot there — but I didn't, I actually got a pain in me arse. He was a member of a band, The Chessmen, and he was always in late. He was a very good bass guitarist and in the early days — the early days — I only lasted three months (laughs) but the roll call would be 'Ballagh?' and I'd say 'Here' so I was Robert Ballagh for about six weeks. Then you go on and find yourself in *The Evening Press*, but that's a tricky one nowadays … And then out of boredom … well I was in the Dublin Shakespeare Society, which is where I met Bob Quinn in a Tyrolean hat and lederhosen, playing the piano and smoking a pipe and that's all he ever did as far as I remember. But that was more Shakespeare.

Oh yeah. 'The Uxorious Nature of Othello' delivered by a guy who was Othello but was also a hypnotherapist — that was a regular house filler. And then there was an academy place in Camden Street … Miles O'Malley O'Donoghue and Ray MacAnally were teaching there with a lot of actors from the Abbey because, frankly, they weren't paid very much. They did elocution lessons and things like that and wherever an actor was teaching these classes that's where they'd be inclined to go for extras, so Des Cave and myself found ourselves doing extra work in the Queen's Theatre. Then it came to a crunch when you'd be doing little bits of parts and they'd put on a play — one of my father's plays which they used to do in those days whenever something flopped — they'd put on the most recent McCann thing and people'd go for a laugh — most of them had been successful and they'd fill for a fortnight or so — T.P. McKenna had gone away to do Stephen D. in London and I don't know what age T.P. was, but I was …

GS: Fifty then was he?

DMcC: I'm saying nothing … but I was a lot younger and some kind of [Ernest] Blythian logic applied that the author's

169

son would be the perfect substitute and I hadn't a clue. I was put into this play which meant that I then had to rehearse full-time which meant that I had to get out of *The Evening Press*. And like most people who don't do anything in Ireland you have to pick something ... I was then an actor. Because I hadn't got a job — it's like authors and filmmakers and poets and ballerinas — if you don't do anything else you can say anything you like really — I think ...

GS: So you did appear in one of your father's plays?

DMcC: I did yeah ...

GS: And was that the only time?

DMcC: No I did one later on — another revival because he didn't write any new ones after I went into the business (laughs).

GS: Not to ask the obvious question, but how did he feel about your going into the business?

DMcC: He never told me really. I think he objected. I don't think he was that keen. On the other hand, he frequently told me early on that if he put his mind to it he would have been twice as good as I was and he was, I believe, a very good actor. He appeared on 2RN — that's early Radio Éireann. He used to write and appear and play. I'm told — and I'm still finding out interesting things about him — that he was actually quite a good actor — very good? He could have been a terrific actor — I've no idea.

GS: You didn't hear any recordings?

DMcC: No, I don't think they had machinery for recordings.

GS: Did young actors then have an attitude to the Abbey the way young actors now have an attitude to the Abbey?

DMcC: I don't know. What is the attitude now?

GS: It's the enemy — the established theatre …

DMcC: Well, at that time it was the only place to go …

GS: Really, yeah …

DMcC: It was the only place you could start really unless you were … Tony Doyle was asked why did he go to England and he said, 'You needed Gaelic to get into the Abbey and for the Gate you needed other qualifications'(laughs). And he didn't have either of those.

GS: He could have made the effort … to learn Irish (laughs). What was your first film? Was it the first film I ever saw you in, *The Fighting Prince of Donegal*? I was about seven or eight when I saw it and you were about fifteen or sixteen?

DMcC: I was twenty.

GS: It must have been a big thing at the time?

DMcC: It was huge, yeah. It was also outside Ireland. Maybe I had been in something else because everyone got into something in the summertime you know, but that was serious. I mean it was Walt Disney and Walt Disney at that time was very, very big and so just the idea of being picked and to do it… yeah, it was amazing. But in the end it was no big deal, you know.

171

GS: Well, indeed, but how did it come about — were there agents in town in those days?

DMcC: There was one agent in town, Tommy O'Connor. Michael O'Herlihy was directing it and he, fair enough, wanted as many genuine Irish people as possible, and he had Peter McEnery who was contracted with Disney. I think maybe that was his last film — I'm not sure — but he was Red Hugh O'Donnell and he had two other guys in a cell with him and one of them turned out to be an English guy, Tom Adams … he was very good. Pat Laffan and myself went to London to test at Pinewood for these two parts and I went into the agent — Tommy's — shortly afterwards to see what was the result, and he was on the phone. When he got off the phone he said, 'No you didn't get the part' and I said 'Well did Pat get the part?' and he said, 'No, but they want you to play his part' and that was awful really. I'm glad to say I rang him up and asked him would he mind — and I still would. So that was a slightly unsavoury entry into this part-time work that I do — but the Disney thing was interesting — it was a good start, the studios…

GS: I'm curious about that thing with yourself and Pat — obviously it's an unpleasant thing when you've a friend but obviously it didn't affect your friendship …

DMcC: Not at all.

GS: But what did it tell you at that stage about how these choices are made and how an actor has to be?

DMcC: I'm sure O'Herlihy would have wanted the two of us, so it taught me that the director in situations like that is not always in control. He has to do a certain amount of what he's

172

told. He's working under contract to Disney as well — and in those days every film was story-boarded — I mean every frame was there and the director just had to make sure it was done properly. If he departed from any one of those little drawings there'd be a conference on the phone when the rushes were seen — 'Why?' I realised that things could go wrong and you weren't really being a louser by taking the other part because the other guy wasn't going to get it anyway so what could you do? So I played it for both of us (laughs)…

GS: And was it a good shoot? It was the first long shoot you'd done, was it?

DMcC: Yeah. Living in the Irish Club, being chauffeured to Pinewood (laughs) … I discovered on the first night — I was in the bar there with Michael O'Herlihy and who'd been there in pre-production and hadn't noticed this. I took a saunter down to the fireplace and there was this plaque over it which said that the 1922 Treaty was signed in this room —because Pinewood was the home of Lord Birkenhead. When Michael saw that he … (Donal raises imaginary glass to his mouth, then flings it) … into the fireplace. The barman came in to see and we explained the significance of this and he did the same (laughs).

Luckily that was a few weeks before we started — we were over for costume fittings or something so we got that out of the way. And that, maybe, is the most interesting thing about *The Fighting Prince of Donegal* (laughs), and a lot of people still don't know that Pinewood was where that document was signed.

GS: Did you start to define for yourself the different acting experiences?

DMcC: Look, I was playing the guy who was meant to be from Co Wicklow and I was very lucky. I didn't have to do any of the butch stuff — my leg was in a leg-iron and while they were making their escape I said, 'Go on. I'd only be a hindrance …' (laughs) The audience in Dublin cheered that bit. It was great and then I stayed around and was slapped around to give information — which I didn't …

GS: You never told …

DMcC: Never said a word. Gordon Jackson was the wicked captain and he was very funny. He was a very pleasant guy and as there was a lot of stuff being shot we'd be on call. He was two dressing rooms down from me and he knew it was my first time so he invited me in for a cup of tea. It was the first time I saw one of those elements that you stick into a mug to make the water boil so we had to do that twice and we'd have our cup of tea and usually had biscuits and things like that. I realised many years later lots of things that he taught me about time wasting — how to use time and not to get bored and to keep thinking about your theatre or whatever. Never to get locked into the idea that this business owns you in any way or that you should be taken in by promises of money or money itself indeed — that certain things are more necessary, and I think that in a way to live a life is more important.

GS: A thought often occurs to me about established people, people who are pursued … but back then there must have been a time when you wondered when the next job was coming or

what way your world would go. Did you feel, 'I don't mind —
it'll happen for me'?

DMcC: Well I don't know what '*happened* for me' means, as
in *something happening* — I mean people died saying 'It
never happened for me' and yet they have happened to
millions of people so I don't know what that means, I really
don't. There's huge truth in clichés as you know, and taking
part is a very good way of spending one's time and trying hard
is very good. But of course early on you don't know what
you're trying to do because you have been sort of summoned
in a certain direction. The theatre was the thing that attracted
me — that's what acting was.

In a sense the cinema was how to get some kind of little
thing isolated maybe in my head — before it became a theatre
idea — and that there must be a common seed of how to
concentrate. In the theatre you build and elaborate on that and
possibly in cinema you try to reduce it a tiny bit if you can. It
occurred to me obviously that you couldn't be throwing your
arms all over the place except in things like *The Nephew*
(laughs) when you'd be asked to do this. Around that time
you're pottering around and you're free and you're working in
England and you're learning how to drink in order to give it up
(laughs) so there's a lot of things ... women ...

GS: You don't even have to ask him about these things ...
Seeing as you brought it up ...

DMcC: You agonised over that didn't you? I'm just saying
that I'm blessed, that I've always considered the thing to be
part of me and so as God takes my life forward he takes these
things forward with me and I would honestly say that only
recently, only in the last ten years or so, I seem to have

clicked. I always regarded myself as a character actor and so I was very fortunate that I never got stuck with the juvenile sticks that were so much a part of theatre plays — just standing there giving the plot with nothing to do. But of course there's another way of looking at that which is maybe — I believe, every character no matter how dull it appears on the page is a character — and so maybe some people were just good at standing there and saying it. But there were some real gooseberries and I never got them — or Mr Blythe knew better than to ask me or to tell me to do it — I never had to play Donal Davoren or Johnny Doyle — thank God (laughs) ...

GS: And did that happen because it happened or did you just fight about those things?

DMcC: I think I must have fought about it, yeah ...

GS: Or you gave off a general impression maybe?

DMcC: I might have, yeah.

GS: I mentioned *The Fighting Prince of Donegal*. Another memory is *The Mad Lomasneys* and I would probably have been astonished at how young you were at that time, but you were already a very established name in Irish people's minds because of film and television and because of those appearances. I'd be curious for you to tell people about *The Mad Lomasneys* because I thought it was a great piece, but it was done of course by English television, wasn't it?

DMcC: Yeah, they were a whole series of short stories — Frank O'Connor and Sean O'Faoláin stories — that were done by Granada and all adapted by Hugh Leonard, brilliantly, and I think there were three series — certainly two series — of them…

GS: But the story is interesting too because it's an example of a young part. This is not an uninteresting juvenile lead and it marks a thing that you specialise in, in terms of your acting, as a very understated noble quality in the acting. Can you tell me a bit about that story …?

DMcC: I can hardly remember it …

GS: Really?

DMcC: Well I do — I remember it because it was the first time I worked with Donald McWhinnie who was a great television director having been a great radio producer/director and a fine piano player. He was really terrific — but he had a great literary sense in the way he got his people working together. I'm sure there are some people around who were in those things. We always became a very good ensemble with a family kind of feeling and the word was good. I mean the absurdity of that guy in *The Mad Lomasneys*, whatever his name was, was the total addiction and the faithfulness and single-mindedness in relation to this girl who didn't care much about him. It was just nice to realise that what you're doing for the story — for the writing — is much more important than having a ball as an actor for the minute. I remember we did a camera run — like a technical run-through — of that and I just walked out impassively. There was a camera waiting as I opened the door to go out — one of these VTR cameras — and I opened the door and just passed through and (hangs his mouth wide open) into the lens and I was right! And someone said afterwards, 'Mr McWhinnie didn't say anything to you about acting the maggot?' and I said, 'I wasn't acting the maggot. I was trying to say that this is what the guy is feeling like but if you don't know that ...', but the cameraman knew it very well because he was having a good old laugh. I enjoyed doing scripts much more than I enjoyed doing parts, you know what I mean? I wouldn't thank you at all for giving me the most wonderful part in a pile of shit — it would mean nothing to me at all ...

GS: But are you any good at judging a script?

DMcC: Yeah, I think so. I think so ... but I was wrong about *Hamlet*! (laughs)

GS: You did get to play *Hamlet* eventually though didn't you, with Ray MacAnally's careful production. Was that a worthwhile experience?

DMcC: The Celtic *Hamlet*. It was worthwhile because I'm still here (laughs). Tomás MacAnna and Ray had often talked about doing a kind of Celtic *Hamlet* and they had a fair idea of what to do but they never got to do it. Then Ray decided to have a go at it and Phyllis Ryan backed it up. But for a week-and-a-half I thought that we were only pretending when we would say 'Something is rotten in the State of Ireland', and we'd say 'Yeah, yeah it'll be okay when we start saying it properly' (laughs). Then towards the end, 'We've come to see you crowned at *Maynooth*' (laughs). Maynooth was instead of Wittenberg where your man was at university and then Hamlet has a perfectly good line where he says, 'Yes, by St Patrick, but there is, Horatio' and of course that used to bring the house down, and it was just an ordinary English swear expression at the time ... and a serious one ...

GS: And the set was of drumlins and things was it?

DMcC: There were little bits of things on wheels that went around. And there was a very good guy who did the costumes and he had to get a certain type of cloth so he was sent to London to get this stuff and at some stage during the rehearsals we got a postcard from the Isle of Man — he had been given the money in cash (laughs). So I became more traditional — I had a black jerkin and tights — the tights we got from Burke's and the black jerkin I got from a lorry driver who was stopped at the lights on Stephen's Green one Saturday afternoon. He was wearing this loose thing and I could see that if you punched holes in it you could, you know, put thongs across and I said, 'How much do you want for that jacket?' and he said, 'A fiver,' and he gave it out to me out the window and I went in to the Gaiety and punched a set of holes

179

down the thing and we got bootlaces — not shoelaces — and I got a white shirt and a jockstrap and a pair of shoes and that was me …

GS: Off you went …

DMcC: It wasn't very Celtic — an Esso Ireland driver — that's Irish enough for me …

GS: It wasn't around the time of this *Hamlet* that drink took hold by any chance was it?

DMcC: Well, that's a fair question, because we rehearsed in the Temperance Club on Gardiner Street and there were lots of statues there with little naggin bottles hidden behind them — I don't know, it never bothered me as it did later …

GS: What year was that *Hamlet*?

DMcC: I don't know, I haven't a clue. But it's not hard to find in the books — it's the only one! (laughs)

GS: We're weaving back and forth but I wanted to ask you about *Philadelphia, Here I Come*, because it's the one example where you did both — did it on stage and did it …

DMcC: Never did it on stage …

GS: Oh really …

DMcC: No …

GS: I never do research …

DMcC: I told you this was the way to approach this …

GS: Absolutely …

(Audience applause and laughter.)

GS: So how did that cast come about … said he recovering hastily (laughs) …

DMcC: I don't know.

GS: Well here's a question that I know we talked about during our extensive research. Why did they not take advantage of film and have the same person play Private and Public Gar?

DMcC: I imagine because of the budget.

GS: It never arose as a notion even?

DMcC: I think there was the idea of making the other character just a voice … in the end it's a very honourable go at it but to translate something that's so essentially theatrical is tricky but they finally sold it — it never got a proper cinema release because of various legal things but Des Cave saw it in a magazine for 'theatre classics' … it's a much-rented thing in the States anyway and a lot of people seem to tape it now because it's in the schools. Even it if wasn't going to translate perfectly into film it was still a great pleasure doing it.

GS: And would it [Gar Public] be your favourite of the two parts?

DMcC: I've no idea. In that kind of production again you're talking about something like Captain Boyle and Joxer and you've got 'public' and 'private', they're essentially two bits of the same person, so the characters become one character, which I find in my own personal way, a play is a character as well. It's just constituent pieces of the whole. Because you know good playwrights don't write — well of course they do, they write line by line and word by word — but they write from an idea that is a character. Otherwise, how do they say 'It's not coming out right?' What's not coming out right? It would be very hard to explain I'm sure but when it does come out right they know, it has something, and maybe the strongest example of that was when I read *The Steward of Christendom* — I mean that play is a character in itself. Sebastian's stuff, like in *Aengus McNulty*, now the person and the writing together create a definite recognisable character and, I don't know, a smell or whatever it is, but it's a sense.

GS: Did you get that feeling the first time you read *The Steward of Christendom*. Did you get it straight away?

DMcC: Oh yeah, I recognised huge chunks of it, having spent a lot of my childhood down in Co Wexford, which turned out to be about, as a crow would fly, ten miles from Kiltegan in Co Wicklow, where I used to spend from April to September on the farm in a place called Monaseed. My mother was born there and I knew that this man in *The Steward of Christendom* had been born on a farm, and his life then was always spent thinking of returning to that. But the writing actually struck me as being the observation of somebody who hadn't been actually born there, but had been privileged to be let into it much more than that. I sensed that immediately and I did think, unworthily for a while, that Sebastian had found out how my formative years had been spent (laughs), but it turned out that he was exactly the same. He spent the whole summer with his aunt, and of course 'a city kid' on a farm, well, he thinks he's discovered all these things, that he's the only person in the whole world who knows where a certain hen lays and things like that … I loved it.

GS: And in loving it, did you also know that you could play it or were you afraid of it?

DMcC: No, no. I had no idea, but I wasn't going to say that to myself because I didn't even know if the whole thing would work, but it became obvious it would only work if you could go at it as though it couldn't fail. And what is failure anyway? But to present that play in a tiny theatre, with Max Stafford-Clark and Sebastian Barry being there and a terrific cast, to find yourself with this extraordinary hit for just doing what you see is necessary to present the play was great. It was weird and strange and …

GS: It was an extraordinarily protracted run even by theatre standards and there was a lot of travel involved …

DMcC: Yeah …

GS: Did you never grow tired of it? Or grow weary of playing it — not with the play, but with the effort …

DMcC: Yeah, I knew I was tired but I think I paced myself pretty well, but I wouldn't have gone on, I think, a day longer than we did.

GS: Really?

DMcC: Yeah, but I do that. I try and say 'No' and I'll do it up to that day, but don't ask me to do an extra three weeks or something like that.

GS: But do you like that about theatre, that notion that you have to re-do it, re-do it, re-find over and over again?

DMcC: Yeah.

GS: Unlike the film, where once it's done, it's gone?

DMcC: Well, it's essential to keep doing something that's really good because perfection is impossible and you know, cliché again, improvement is always possible. But not like the old-fashioned things like the fella who says 'cut out the improvements and get on with the play'. Just a word one night or the shape of a sentence or the tiny difference in the length of a pause or something is amazing to find, a mistake that will work much better than you actually intended and so that becomes one of your 'masterstrokes' (laughs) ... it's absurd and people say 'how did you think of that?' and it's because you couldn't think of anything (laughs) ... because it was Wednesday or something ...!

GS: And a more unworthy thought, just take something like *The Steward of Christendom*, which was a very important performance for you, but did you ever find yourself not giving it the full welly?

DMcC: Oh no, you couldn't do it. That wouldn't work if there was any relaxation in intensity of it, I'm convinced of it. Some people say I should have relaxed, mainly because I was driving them fuckin' mad ... but I think it was worth it, of all the things I did where you would say 'To hell with them I'm going to do this to fuck', that was it (laughs).

GS: Do you think that relates to time and place as well as the thing itself. That it's when it happens for an actor as well as the play itself, like if that play had been handed to you ten or fifteen years ago, it would've been a different thing that you were doing ...

184

DMcC: Oh, absolutely, yeah. I think it's one of those businesses of timing because for somebody of the real age to do Thomas Dunne, I don't think would be … well maybe somebody, some of our famous 'keep fit' people (laughs) …

GS: Sheer stamina?

DMcC: Yes, you want to have the bones of several years on the other side of it in the same way as people playing very young parts should be that little bit older. But this current thing of casting very young people as the right age, it strikes me as not being totally successful and not valid. Betimes, I think when people write about *Romeo and Juliet* — there's a man sitting from great experience — and our suspension of disbelief is if somebody comes on in, possibly a toupee, but gives you a decent Romeo (laughs), rather than have a fourteen-year-old, who, no matter how good they are, is going to be at the end of a three-week run or whatever still trying to get the actual words … you know the delivery and everything like that. But you can steal that veracity in many ways on film.

GS: Did you ever play a part where you later thought, 'I wish that had come to me earlier, it was the wrong time for me. I did a good job of it but it was the wrong time for me'?

DMcC: No, I don't believe that, because one thing I decided last week, for some reason or other, I don't know why, was that the expression of somebody 'being born out of his time' is rubbish because people are born 'in their time'. Isn't that true? (laughs) I think it's silly and this bloody thing of 'What he would have been if he'd only hung on a few years (laughs) … if he'd hung on before the shares went up, you know he could have died from the drink.' Oh yeah, and what did he die of? Ah, the drink! You know when people say 'What would

Brendan Behan have written if he hadn't drunk so much?' If he hadn't drunk at all he mightn't have written anything! I don't make jokes about drinking because I don't find it funny, but at the same time, I can't deny having done a lot of it and in this beautiful city and county, probably at my prime (laughs). It's stupid because it sounds like you're encouraging people to go and have a go at it and see if you survive — then you might be a very good actor. But I do know that having been the kind of person I am, with the kind of behaviour and indulgence in alcohol that I went on with, but having by the grace of God got away from it … But that means, by extension or implication, that it was worth having something to get away from which sounds a bit silly and I don't in any way mean to say, be a reformed drunk, and you suddenly become brilliant or something like that … it's not true …

GS: Is it like having been a Catholic?

Pause.

DMcC: Well, nobody made me drink … (laughs)

GS: I could tell how pleased you were to talk about *The Steward of Christendom*. What about Brian Friel, and is there a similar relationship?

DMcC: Yeah, I just love writing. I think the actor's job is to serve writing, that is the job. It's not self-advertisement, it's not dressing up, it's not passing the time, it's not doing a job that's less boring than the one your parents wanted you to do, it's about treating as serious what somebody has gone through an awful lot of time to produce and what you think is wonderful writing. Then, for the theatre and for the cinema too, to be able to help to make that happen, the essential

186

change from being there on the page to being, as it were, 'standing up' rather than being the book lying open; to make that happen, to be able to feel that you can and fulfil an author's expectations to a certain extent. I'm sure nobody ever does it perfectly, I certainly couldn't, but that is wonderful, and for a writer to just say that you were near, you know, is huge satisfaction for me.

GS: And on the Brian Friel plays, everybody remembers *Faith Healer*. I remember when I was up in your flat seeing a poster hanging over the fireplace ...

DMcC: That's the only one.

GS: That's the only one, yeah?

DMcC: That's because it doesn't say *Faith Healer* on it. It's just the first pull of a poster by Robert Ballagh which he gave to me the second time I did it. It looks good and it's a conversation piece, except nobody ever comes round to see me, except the odd, the odd ...

GS: The odd interviewer?

DMcC: Yeah, that was *Faith Healer* ... I actually stopped drinking for the length of that and for the first time seriously said, 'I can't'. Well Joe Dowling agreed with me, or indeed maybe I came round to agreement with Joe Dowling, that working and drinking didn't go together and I don't mean just during the daytime or anything, I mean just pack it in completely while you're doing it. So I had a good ten years of going along like that, there's no point in pretending that the two things aren't linked ... I was terrified the first time I did *Faith Healer*, absolutely terrified because I'd been away from the theatre and I'd spent a lot of time in London doing a lot of TV that frankly anybody could have done. But it was a bad and dangerous time when you could have ended up doing those lumpy, lemony, thirtyish, gobshites (laughs) … Over there they weren't that keen to take you on as a character actor, it's so sub-divided. So, when that came I was staggered that I was asked to do it having been off the map completely and I was very grateful that people like Joe and Brian thought I was the right person because I certainly didn't have a very high opinion of myself and that was mixed in with all sorts of things happening within my family at the time.

It was a hugely traumatic time and I'll never forget the end of the first night in the Abbey when someone had sort of rung up at a strange hour — someone I really didn't want to think about — to say they were going to be in the audience, and it was threatening. Anyway, I said I'm going to have to do this, I can't chicken out. I did it very deliberately and I had this thing — which I have since taken into my way of performing — which is that if this is the last thing you ever do, make sure it's good. And the first thirty-five minutes of *Faith Healer* is Frank on his own, and I did it and I enjoyed it on a level I'd never been on before. I found myself on a level of being so confident and I was being comforted by the thing I was doing in an extraordinary way. I just played it straight down with the pauses … looking for something … trying to think of the right word. I used to take very long pauses and do that kind of thing (stares around audience). And the person who had rung up and frightened me sent me a letter saying 'How did you know exactly where I was sitting?' (laughs) and we're very friendly ever since. Thank God. It was a member of my family.

But the end of that first piece — 'We'll come to that later', 'Indeed' or something like that — and I just go off and the lights black out and there was terrific applause because it was the end of an act, but I suddenly got an extraordinary feeling … the stage was blacked off, it was quite a small stage and the walk from the edge of the stage to the door of the stage area was long and very dimly lit, especially having been out there for half-an-hour and I suddenly got hit with this ice-cold thing here (slaps the right side of his neck) and a red hot thing here (slaps the left side of his neck) and I didn't know what was going on and it was Dr Friel with his G&T and his lips (big laugh). And I sort of advanced a stage that night, I think.

GS: Did you like being on stage alone?

DMcC: Yeah, dangerously so I think, (laughs) I did … I would think that if you had to say, 'Did anything make me think that I could get myself round *The Steward of Christendom*?', it was having done *Faith Healer*. Certainly it's great, it's such a terrific piece of writing.

GS: Yeah, you could see how it would …

DMcC: Yeah, it's lovely, I mean, I link them together very much.

GS: I asked the question because it did strike me that there's a curious thing about being alone on stage … I mean obviously there's a certain egotistical value to it but it's more a question of watching an actor and wondering is the actor comfortable being alone on stage, comfortable being exposed …

DMcC: If you're doing the work you want to do, then you're on stage with something you love so you're not alone at all. And not to forget that if your work is good and if your approach to it is right, you will hopefully leave your ego at home or miles away from the theatre. You're doing this work, you're there, people are looking at you, you're doing the work of somebody who's responsible. You love the stuff you're doing, you want it to come through you and I mean you just cannot be selfish, if the work you're doing is so good. It can't come into it, you mustn't put yourself between the work and people doing it. Although you're physically there I like to think sometimes that if you can find the voice that the writer has for the character (which he wouldn't be able to tell you) … if you can find that and rehearse and rehearse and keep it and do it and do it and do it until you say 'Yes' and it is going through and you do find sometimes the play has gone a bit ahead of you as an actor. I don't mean becoming the character … that's all bullshit — to be a vehicle for good writing is a great privilege and I think, well I know, that God is a great help and I think the theatre can be calm at times. It certainly has been — for me — a most revealing, spiritual place.

GS: I have to ask about Bob Quinn because he's running the TV cameras here today, but it is another kind of collaboration that you've been involved in at the film end of things also. How does that kind of collaboration work? I suppose there is no script at that point or is there?

DMcC: I was never sure because the first one was in Irish (laughs). Ah no that's not true — that's a cheap shot. As far as I remember there wasn't when we agreed *Poitín*, it hadn't been fully scripted. I should stand to be corrected.

BQ: You're right …

DMcC: Thank you! Because I think the thing was to make sure we got a cast and so Bob arrives in The Two Sisters and we talked about it and he was talking about the two salesmen and the poitín maker and how to get Cyril, and the obvious way to get Cyril Cusack to do it was to — even then Bob wouldn't be as cynical as me — but the best way to get Cyril would be to tell him that Niall Toibin was doing it (laughs) and he might get Toibin if he told him that I was going to do it and to tell Toibin that I would do it if he did it. It was something like that, wasn't it? It worked out anyway and everybody wanted to be in the first feature film *as gaeilge*, in colour and it was great, it was real 'moviemaking' and that was terrific.

GS And then *Budawanny*?

DMcC: Yeah. We didn't have to say anything at all the first time doing that, it was great. Bottles of stout and move your lips. That introduced me to Clare Island and that's a splendid place, as anyone who's been there knows. And Neil Jordan. I've been in two or three of his, but the first, *Angel*, you got the pages every so often and I hadn't a clue who the character I was playing was. But it didn't bother me and I was thrilled to find out, when I went to see it, that I was a villain! (laughs) Well, I actually figured that I was the villain because on the last day's work Ray MacAnally shot me in the back (laughs) and I'd a gun in my hand, so I knew I was the nasty bit.

GS: It strikes me as you talk about Neil Jordan and Bob Quinn, that it wouldn't be everybody that you treat that way…

DMcC: How do you mean?

GS: That if somebody came up to you and said, 'Would you make a film with me?', it wouldn't be everybody you'd say yes to, so what is it makes you say yes?

DMcC: The script and the …

GS: But where there is no script and there's only Bob Quinn or Neil Jordan or whatever, is there something that makes you want to do it apart from the writing?

DMcC: Well, yeah, I like anybody who'll come up and say, 'Do you want to do it — have a go — do you want to join in — let's do it!' But I wouldn't say yes straight away … anymore! (laughs)

GS: Ah, go on …

DMcC: But I know that I found a script that he (indicates Gerry Stembridge) left behind the sofa the other day (laughs)

GS: Ah, so you're not going to tell us what it is?

DMcC: With the Dun Laoghaire students, I love to do one of them every so often, but I don't think everybody should start queuing, because, not that I ever objected, but people will try to take you for a sucker … I'd rather take the chance of somebody else thinking I was a sucker because if I do it with the right intentions, there's no way I am a sucker. You can get very sincere people who want to do it and I say, I don't like the script, or I've seen it before, or why just do something that we've seen one hundred times and how is it going to benefit just by setting it in … Kinnegad or whatever. When you find people trying to promote themselves. That's not what I want to do. I would like to promote something like *The Nephew*, Eugene Brady's first film and I'd even share the jet with Pierce Brosnan to go around and publicise that (laughs). But in the end you just make the decision and I suppose you make some wrong ones. But then you turn down something and then somebody turns around and says 'Look it made so much money' — Well so feckin' what (laughs). If it's still bad. We do know that a lot of rubbish makes money. The bigger the boat, the more money you get (laughs).

GS: I'm supposed to take questions from the audience and I better do it soon, but was that sufficiently tangential for you?

DMcC: Yeah … what was the tangent from? (laughs)

GS: I don't know … As you look to the future, for example *The Steward of Christendom*, do you see yourself, if given the opportunity, taking on a theatre role as strenuous as that again or would you prefer the more concentrated film projects that will begin and end within a period of time?

DMcC: Well, at the moment I'm still tired from the theatre and I haven't been that well. So I'm very glad to have had nearly a year away, although I went and did a picture with John Turturro which was going to be shown here but the distributors or something went …

GS: *Illuminata* …

DMcC: Yeah, *Illuminata*, I enjoyed that … But there again a fella says 'We have no money, will you come to New York' and so you go and it turns out to be New Jersey — for Christ's sake! That was great, very enjoyable (laughs) but I don't really want to do anything and it's not that I feel I deserve but I do think I need a rest. But I think anything in the form of a theatre script at the moment would disappoint me if I'm still this close to Sebastian's play, because of the length of time I was with it and tied up with it and committed to it, so I don't know … I know I'm also speaking as a tired fellow so these things are changeable. Funnily enough, this is a kind of retrospective

193

about one's life in the cinema but I've been a total wanderer into the cinema. I never set out to have a career. I've just been available for people. I must say I was staggered to find that such a thing as a retrospective was being planned and I presumed it meant over an afternoon and an evening because I couldn't think of enough films to fill out more than a day anyway.

But now I would actually like not to sit on anything but just leave the theatre for a little while and just see what I could do with your Turturro's and 'Nouveau Quinns' and (laughs) you know, I'm not in a rush because I worked so hard for that length of time and I did *The Nephew* and I did another picture, all small-budget things but with my standard of living I never get to spend the money, so I'm not in a panic to do anything and I am, as I sit here, not ambitious for anything really.

GS: Grand, grand. Thank you very much — this evening you've made my life very easy for me and it was a fantastic pleasure. Thank you.

DMcC: Not at all.

(Leaves stage to applause.)

Gerry Stembridge is a writer and director.

Image from page 179: line drawing by Donal inspired by Celtic Hamlet.

Donald Taylor Black

Donal McCann (1943-99)

From *Film Ireland*, Issue 72, August/September 1999.

Eight days after Donal's death, I am writing this in a room with a framed poster of the Gate production of *Juno and the Paycock* on one wall. Geraldine Plunkett, as Juno, stands behind Donal, her left hand on his left shoulder; Donal, as Captain Boyle, sits on a kitchen chair, with his right elbow resting on a table, his right hand supporting the side of his face and the Captain's nautical cap on his left thigh. His eyes are looking directly at me.

I was not a close friend but admired his work on stage and screen for almost thirty years, knew him for over twenty and worked with him on a number of occasions. The most recent time was February 1999, when he recorded the narration for my documentary about Viking archaeology, *Down to the Bedrock*, which I believe was the last work he undertook.

At the time of writing there has been a week of tributes, both spoken and written: from the usual clichés, hagiography and lazy journalistic guff that follows a death, particularly a premature one, to the real thing from people who know. After the pious revisionism of a couple of priests, who concelebrated the requiem mass in the chapel of Terenure College, had not only begun the process of canonisation — at which Donal would have snorted in disbelief — but also airbrushed his former longtime partner, Fedelma Cullen, out of history, it was appropriate that Kevin Myers unleashed the full force of his military firepower three days later in the Irishman's Diary column of *The Irish Times*. Fergus Linehan wrote a sensitive and intelligent piece in the same newspaper, as did Hugh Leonard in the *Sunday Independent*, and I was touched by the memories of Donal recalled by fellow actors Gabriel Byrne and Barry McGovern in the Irish edition of the *Sunday Times*. I was especially moved, however, by a splendid contribution from his loyal friend, Pat Laffan, in *The Sunday Business Post*.

Since Donal's death, I took another look at a documentary I made in 1993, *From Ballybeg to Broadway*, which I hadn't seen since it was first shown. It follows the rehearsals and openings in Dublin and New York of Brian Friel's play, *Wonderful Tennessee*. Donal played the part of an apparently successful bookie (!) called Terry, wearing a Panama hat for most of the show, but I had forgotten how important was the character of George, a performer — in this case a musician — who is dying of cancer. Seeing the film again, though, there are several images of Donal that are typical of the man: peering over his bifocals at the first reading, or eating a sandwich as he sat in his vest on opening night in his Abbey dressing room. But the one that stood out for me was Donal, with fellow cast members, amongst the dark shadows in the wings of the Plymouth Theatre on Broadway, ready to go onstage for the curtain call. He literally sprang up the steps as he went out into the bright light.

Back in mid-January, when I was deep in the post-production of *Down to the Bedrock*, I was thinking of a suitable voice to narrate it. As we had already recorded Seamus Heaney reading two sections of his poem, 'Viking Dublin: Trial Pieces', I felt we needed not only a Dublin voice but the best Dublin voice possible. I briefly hesitated about Donal because I was very much aware of how ill he had been for some time, although on the last occasion I had spoken to Paul Durcan he had told me that Donal was in good form and confounding the doctors. Slightly nervously, I telephoned Pat Laffan to ask for his opinion. Pat said that he thought that Donal might be physically able to do it but had no idea whether he would be interested or not. Pat gave me Donal's telephone number and I left a message on the answering machine. Donal rang me back later that day and, to my delight, immediately agreed to do it. 'Fax me the script as soon as you can,' he said.

We were mixing the sound in Moynihan Russell's on Monday, 1 February and I had told Donal that it would suit us if he could come in towards late afternoon, early evening. I rang him at lunchtime and said that I would send a taxi to collect him at his apartment so as to get him to Herbert Street for 5 p.m. He said that as the weather was sunny, he would like to walk along the canal from Harold's Cross, and this plan would also allow him to make a diversion via Chatham Street to buy some fish. 'Fish is all I can eat,' he said.

After he had done the job, even more brilliantly than I had expected, he chatted with sound mixer, Tony Russell, my editor, Mossie Healy, and myself. He seemed particularly pleased that Bertolucci had agreed to do an interview for the documentary that Bob Quinn was making about him. Just before Donal left, Mossie quietly asked him if he would mind signing his programme of *The Steward of Christendom*. Donal put pen to paper, with a smile on his face. 'Do you know when was the last time someone asked me to sign one of these?' We didn't. 'When I was being wheeled into the operating theatre to have part of my pancreas removed, the surgeon handed me the programme and a pen. I said to him, "Can you not wait till after the operation?" "I'd rather you did it, now," he replied.' His timing was as sharp as ever. We laughed, although feeling guilty inside. I walked him downstairs to the front door. 'Where's me fish?' I handed him the brown paper parcel and he wished me good luck before setting off along Herbert Street in the direction of Baggot Street Bridge.

Donald Taylor Black is a film maker and writer.

Drawing by Donal of himself as Captain Boyle of *Juno and the Paycock*, featuring Terenure College stripes in the background.

Ronan Wilmot

A Reminisce

The first film I acted in was called *The Hard Way*. It was shot in Ardmore Studios and the environs of Bray. It starred Lee Van Cleef, Patrick McGoohan, Edna O'Brien, John Cowley, Donal McCann and myself. The year was 1979 and, believe me, a dog walking across the studio's car park would have been cause for comment in those days. Nothing happened in Irish film at that time — nothing.

Suffice to say the film was completed after two directors had been replaced, and the 'wrap' party consisted of one bottle of whiskey donated by Patrick McGoohan.

A week or so later I was walking towards Trinity College after purchasing my air ticket to London, when I bumped into Donal.

'Howya Head, what are you up to?' he asked me.

'Just bought a ticket to London, heading over for a few days'.

'I'll go with you,' he said.

And so I spent the most amazing five days in his company, staying at the Irish Club in Eaton Square — breakfast at nine o'clock in the basement dining room, then on to the Chelsea Drugstore on the Kings Road for ten-thirty — playing pool, drinking champagne and orange juice. All afternoon we spent in the drinking club the Kismet, with artists, actors, criminals, and Special Branch 'heads', before a Chinese meal in Gerard Street and the remainder of the evening back at the Irish Club.

One afternoon Donal said, 'Come with me. I am going to introduce you to my agent', and so I ascended the rickety Soho stairs of Peter Crouch's agency and walked in. Donal announced: 'This is Ronan Wilmot and you are to take him on.'

A quiet, decisive, generous, helpful man was Donal McCann.

Ronan Wilmot is an actor.

**Oration by Professor John Luce at the graduation
ceremony in which Donal was awarded an honorary
doctorate by Trinity College, Dublin.**

*Orationes in Comitus Aestivis Posterioribus
Habitae Termino SS. Triniatis Die Undecimo
Julii MCMXCVII*

Doctor in Letters Donal Francis John McCann

Members of the University, it seems a long time since your
Orator has had the chance to present an Irish actor or actress. I
might remind you of certain famous names like Siobhán and
Cyril, stars of the stage whom we honoured in the past, and
whose fame still lives in our land. And so it is with much
pleasure that I now introduce Donal Francis John McCann, a
shining ornament of the contemporary Irish theatre. Theatre
business was certainly part of his family life in childhood, for
a number of his father's comedies had been staged at the
Abbey. In 1962 he himself joined the Abbey company, that
famous nursery of theatrical achievement, and soon began to
delight Dublin audiences with his exceptional talent. Round
after round of applause resounded in his ears when he played
Captain Boyle in *Juno and the Paycock*, or took part with
Peter O'Toole in *Waiting for Godot*. The role of Frank Hardy
in Brian Friel's *Faith Healer* was not an easy one, but he
carried it off to perfection. He has also excelled in film parts,

202

notably under John Huston's direction as Gabriel Conroy in *The Dead*. When he treads the boards his presence has an almost supernatural quality, so strong and mesmeric is his hold over the audience. Horace's phrase about 'force under firm control' seems very applicable to his acting style, particularly in relation to his recent portrayal of an elderly retired policeman, a performance of such virtuosity that the hard-boiled critics of Broadway were moved to offer him the accolade of 'actor supreme'. Today in our College theatre he has a non-speaking part, but were he to utter those famous words, 'What is the moon? What is the stars?', you might well be moved to reply, 'You are one of them'. Rumour has it that Donal does not smile easily, but if you smile kindly on him, perhaps he will return the compliment. I at least, like a Roman stage-manager, strongly urge you to give him a strong ovation.

Johannes Victor Luce, Orator Publicus
Public Orator

Selected Theatre Credits

(In order of year, play, playwright, company, theatre)

1963 *The Successor*, R. Raffalt, The Abbey, The Abbey

1963 *Put a Beggar on Horseback*, J McCann, The Abbey, The Abbey

1963 *Flann agus Clemintin*, Pantomime, The Abbey, The Abbey

1964 *The Man from Clare*, J.B. Keane, The Abbey, The Abbey

1964 *The Wooing of Duvesa*, M.J. Molloy, The Abbey, The Abbey

1964 *Thomas Muskerry*, P. Colum, The Abbey, The Abbey

1964 *The Big Long Bender*, S. Love, The Abbey, The Abbey

1964 *Aisling as Tír-na- nÓg*, Pantomime, The Abbey, The Abbey

1965 *Church Street*, L. Robinson, The Abbey, The Abbey

1965 *Cathleen Ní Houlihan*, W.B. Yeats, The Abbey, The Abbey

1965 *A Jew Called Sammy*, J. McCann, The Abbey, The Abbey

1965 *The Best of Motives*, S. Dowling, The Abbey, The Abbey

1965 *Drama at Inish Eirí na Gealaí*, L. Robinson/Gregory, The Abbey,
The Abbey

1965 *Emer agus an Laoch*, Pantomime, The Abbey, The Abbey

1966 *Yerma*, F.G. Lorca, The Abbey, The Abbey

1966 *The Call*, Tom Coffey, The Abbey, The Abbey

1966 *The Singer*, P. Pearse, The Abbey, The Abbey

1966 (July) *The Plough and The Stars*, S. O' Casey, The Abbey, The Abbey

1966 *One for the Grave*, L. MacNeice, The Abbey, The Abbey

1966 *Death Is for Heroes*, M. Judge, The Abbey, The Abbey

1966 (Nov) *The Plough and the Stars*, S. O' Casey, The Abbey, The Abbey

1966 *Tarry Flynn*, P. Kavanagh/P.J. O' Connor, The Abbey, The Abbey

1966 *Fernando agus an Ríon Óg*, Pantomime, The Abbey, The Abbey

1967 (Jan) *The Shaughraun*, D. Boucicault, The Abbey, The Abbey

1967 (July) *The Shaughraun*

1967 *From Inniskeen to Baggot St Bridge*, Tribute to Kavanagh,
The Abbey, The Abbey

1968 *Riders to the Sea*, J.M. Synge, The Abbey The Abbey

1968 *The Au Pair Man*, H. Leonard, Gemini, The Gate

1969 *She Stoops to Conquer*, O. Goldsmith, The Abbey, The Abbey

1969 *A Crucial Week in the Life of a Grocer's Assistant*, T. Murphy,
The Abbey, The Abbey

1969 *Waiting for Godot*, S. Beckett, The Abbey, The Abbey

1969 as above, Royal Court

1969 *Man and Superman*, G.B. Shaw, Gaiety

1969 *Prayer for my Daughter*, T. Babe, Royal Court

1970 *The Dumb Waiter*, H. Pinter, The Abbey, The Peacock
1970 *The Hostage*, B. Behan, The Abbey, The Abbey
1972 *Miss Julie*, A. Strindberg, RSC, The Place, London
1973 *Hamlet*, W. Shakespeare, Gemini, Gaiety
1973 *Absurd Person Singular*, A. Ayckbourn, Gate
1976 *Tea and Sex and Shakespeare*, T. Kilroy, The Abbey, The Abbey
1980 *The Blue Macushla*, T. Murphy, The Abbey, The Abbey
1980 *The Shadow of a Gunman*, S. O'Casey, The Abbey, The Abbey
1980 *Faith Healer*, B. Friel, The Abbey, The Abbey
1981 *The Shadow of a Gunman* (American Tour)
1981 *Night and Day*, T. Stoppard, The Abbey, The Abbey
1986 *Juno and the Paycock*, S. O'Casey, The Gate
1983 *The Plough and The Stars*, S. O'Casey, The Gaiety
1988 *Translations*, B. Friel, The Gaiety
1991 *A Life*, H. Leonard, The Olympia
1993 *Da*, H. Leonard, The Olympia
1993 *Wonderful Tennessee*, B. Friel, The Abbey, The Abbey
1995 *The Steward of Christendom*, S. Barry, Royal Court

Donal McCann Filmography

The Fighting Prince of Donegal
(Michael O'Herlihy, 1966)
As Sean O'Toole

Sinful Davey
(John Huston, 1968)
As Sir James Graham

Philadelphia Here I Come
(John Quested, 1970)
As Gar (Public)

Miss Julie
(John Glenister/Robin Phillips, 1972)
As Jean

The Mackintosh Man
(John Huston, 1973)
As 1st Fireman

Poitín
(Bob Quinn, 1978)
As Labhcás, Michil's Agent

Angel
(Neil Jordan, 1982)
As Bonner

Reflections
(Kevin Billington, 1983)
As Edward Lawless

Cal
(Pat O'Connor, 1984)
As Shamie McCluskie

Out of Africa
(Sydney Pollack, 1985)
As Doctor

Mr. Love
(Roy Battersby, 1985)
As Leo

Rawhead Rex
(George Pavlou, 1986)
As Tom Garron

Budawanny
(Bob Quinn, 1987)
As Priest
Also credited as:
Consultant Director

The Dead
(John Huston, 1987)
As Gabriel Conroy

High Spirits
(Neil Jordan, 1988)
As Eamon

December Bride
(Thaddeus O'Sullivan, 1990)
As Hamilton Echlin

Saints and Scholars [short]
(Eamonn Manning, 1990)
As Father Ryan

The Miracle
(Neil Jordan, 1991)
As Sam Coleman

The Bargain Shop
(Johnny Gogan, 1992)
Narrator

The Bishop's Story
(Bob Quinn, 1994)
As Bishop/Priest
Also credited as:
Consultant Director

Halcyon Days
(Patrick Dewolf, 1995)
As Joe Green

Stealing Beauty
(Bernardo Bertolucci, 1996)
As Ian Grayson

The Serpent's Kiss
(Philippe Rousselot, 1997)
As The Doctor

Illuminata
(John Turturro, 1998)
As Pallenchio

The Nephew
(Eugene Brady, 1998)
As Tony Egan

Donal McCann Television Credits

Stage Irishman [Documentary]
(Kieran Hickey, 1968)
B.A.C. Films for BBC
Featured as cast member of
Abbey Theatre production of
The Shaughraun in documentary
about Dion Boucicault

Young Man In Trouble
(James Gatward, 1970)
Thames Television
As Frank

*The Sinners: The Mad
Lomasneys*
(Donald McWhinnie, 1970)
Granada Television
As Ned Lowry

The Sinners: One Man, One Boat, One Girl
(Donald McWhinnie, 1971)
Granada Television
As T.J.

Two Gallants
(Gavin Millar, 1972)
BBC
As Corley

Stephen D.
(Donald McWhinnie, 1972)
BBC
As Stephen Dedalus

The Shadow Of A Gunman
(Alvin Rakoff, 1973)
BBC
As Seumas Shields

The Pallisers
(various directors, 1974)
BBC: 26-part series
As Phineas Finn

The Wood Demon
(Donald McWhinnie, 1974)
BBC
As Theodore

Thriller: Screamer
(Shaun O'Riordan, 1975)
ATV
As Jeff Holt

Your Man from the Six Counties
(Barry Davis, 1976)
BBC
As Danny

The Burke Enigma
(Brian Mac Lochlainn, 1978)
RTÉ. 6-part series
As Joe Burke

The Hard Way
(Michael Dryhurst, 1979)
I.T.C.
As Ryan

Katie — The Year of a Child
(Barry Davis, 1979)
BBC
As Big Jim Collins

Visitors
(Peter Ormrod, 1980)
RTÉ
As John Kinsella

Strumpet City
(Tony Barry, 1980)
RTÉ: 7-part series
As Mulhall

The Silver Tassie
(Brian Mac Lochlainn, 1980)
RTÉ/BBC
As Teddy Foran

Sean: Episode 12 — Comrades
(Louis Lentin, 1981)
RTÉ
As Seumas Shields [in original
Abbey production of *The
Shadow of A Gunman*]

The Lost Hour
(Sean Cotter, 1982)
RTÉ
As Sergeant Moran

The Key
(Tony Barry, 1983)
RTÉ
As Sergeant Moran

Access To The Children
(Tony Barry, 1984)
RTÉ /Channel Four
As Malcolmson

Summer Lightning
(Paul Joyce, 1985)
RTÉ/Channel Four
As Dr Lestrange

Tuesday's Child
(Robin Midgley, 1985)
BBC
As Father Doyle

John Huston and The Dubliners
[Doc.] (Lilyan Sievernich, 1987)
Featured as cast member in
documentary about the making
of *The Dead*

*Juno In Jerusalem — The Gate
In Israel*
[Doc.] (Louis Lentin, 1987)
RTÉ
Featured as cast member in
documentary about *Juno and the
Paycock* at the Israel Festival

Who Bombed Birmingham?
(Michael Beckham, 1990)
Granada Television
As "X" — First Bomb Planter

The Donner Party
[Doc.] (Ric Burns, 1992)
Steeplechase Films for
WGBH/WNET
(Voice only)

Force Of Duty
(Pat O'Connor, 1992)
RTÉ/BBC NI
As Simpson Gabby

Hedda Gabler
(Deborah Warner, 1993)
BBC
As Judge Brack

From Ballybeg to Broadway
[Doc.] (Donald Taylor Black,
1993)
Ferndale Films for RTÉ/BBC NI
Featured in documentary about
the first production of *Wonderful
Tennessee*

*Peak Practice: Chance
Encounter*
(Alan Grint, 1994)
Central Independent Television
As Michael

Into The Fire
(Jane Howell, 1995)
BBC: 3-part series
As Frank Candy

Down to the Bedrock
[Doc.] (Donald Taylor Black,
1999)
Poolbeg Productions for RTÉ
Narrator

It Must Be Done Right
[Doc.] (Bob Quinn, 1999)
De Facto Films for RTÉ/Bord
Scannán na hÉireann
Subject of tribute documentary,
based around public interview at
1998 Galway Film Fleadh

*Filmography and television credits compiled by
Donald Taylor Black*